Indigenous Dispossession

Indigenous Dispossession

Housing and Maya Indebtedness in Mexico

M. Bianet Castellanos

Stanford University Press

Stanford, California

STANFORD UNIVERSITY PRESS
Stanford, California

Printed in the United States of America on acid-free, archival-quality paper

Library of Congress Cataloging-in-Publication Data
Names: Castellanos, María Bianet, author.
Title: Indigenous dispossession : housing and Maya indebtedness in Mexico / M. Bianet Castellanos.
Description: Stanford, California : Stanford University Press, 2020. | Includes bibliographical references and index.
Identifiers: LCCN 2020025593 (print) | LCCN 2020025594 (ebook) | ISBN 9781503603288 (cloth) | ISBN 9781503614345 (paperback) | ISBN 9781503614352 (epub)
Subjects: LCSH: Mayas—Housing—Mexico—Cancún. | Housing policy—Mexico—Cancún. | Debt—Mexico—Cancún. | Mayas—Mexico—Cancún—Economic conditions. | Mayas—Urban residence—Mexico—Cancún. | Mayas—Mexico—Cancún—Social conditions.
Classification: LCC F1435.3.H58 C37 2020 (print) | LCC F1435.3.H58 (ebook) | DDC 972/.67—dc23
LC record available at https://lccn.loc.gov/2020025593
LC ebook record available at https://lccn.loc.gov/2020025594

Cover design: Rob Ehle
Cover photo: Self-help housing in a *region* in Cancún. Photograph by the author.
Typeset by BookComp, Inc. in 11/13.5 Adobe Garamond Pro

Para el pueblo de "Kuchmil": Dios bo'otik ti' tulakalile'ex

En memoria de José Asunción Poot Poot (1972–2020)
y Lorenza Poot y Tamay (1948–2020)

And for David, Ben, and Lucía

Contents

Acknowledgments

I begin by acknowledging Maya *pueblos* and their ongoing struggles for land rights and social justice. The pueblo of Kuchmil (a pseudonym) and its diasporic community in Cancún has my everlasting gratitude for sharing their stories and lives with me.

I would like to acknowledge the lands I have occupied. My family hails from the Mexican states of Colima and Michoacán, the land of Otomí, Nahua, Tarasco, and P'urhepecha peoples. I was raised on the land of Chowchilla, Miwok, and Mono peoples in the San Joaquin Valley of California. I currently live on the traditional homelands of Dakota people.

My parents held a special relationship to land as members of an *ejido* (communal landholding) in the sierra of Colima. My uncles and cousins remain members of this ejido. After my father immigrated to the United States, my mother carried on working the land with the help of her young sons. She was granted ejido membership in her own right, a rare feat for women in the 1970s. When my family joined my father to work as migrant farmworkers in California, my parents' relationship to the land reflected their status as cheap, expendable labor. They worked tirelessly to forge another kind of bond to land to replace the home they gave up. We eventually settled in Madera, California, where they purchased an acre of land. My mother tended fifty rosebushes and my father cultivated a wide variety of trees—pomegranate, plum, grapefruit, peach, mulberry, lemon, and walnut. They grew sugarcane, tomatoes, corn, and vegetables, grazed a calf or two, and raised chickens and pigs. Our home became a second home to my relatives who sought work in *el Norte*. My family's struggle to belong as we straddled the tense cultural, political, and economic divide between Mexico and the United States continually shapes the work I do. My maternal grandparents, Lázaro and Isabel, were my first teachers and will always hold a special place in my heart.

I am forever grateful to my siblings—Elsa, Evelia, Efrain, Gumaro, Phillip, Alma, Ari, Isabel, and Fred—and their families for reminding me what matters and for welcoming me home every time. The San Joaquin Valley was dealt a brutal blow after the housing bubble collapsed in 2008. Some of my family members work in real estate and had to grapple with losing their homes and their jobs. This loss also shaped this book.

David Karjanen truly made this book possible. I am blessed to have him in my life. My children, Ben and Lucía, are daily wonders with poetic souls. With them, I see trees punching the air, dinosaurs in diners, and endless possibilities. My father-in-law, Edward Karjanen, recently passed away. He is sorely missed. Raised by a widowed mother during the Great Depression, he loved to tell the story of how his Finnish grandmother Sofia saved his home. We carry his stories with us. For their unwavering support, I thank Louise Karjanen and Ned Karjanen. Kitty kept me company while I wrote.

My editors, Michelle Lipinski and Kate Wahl, and the staff at Stanford University Press were wonderful. I am beholden to Michelle for encouraging me every step of the way. She read my words with great care and, in a sense, *willed* this project to completion. Thank you for believing in me and in this story. I thank freelancer Beth Chapple for her remarkable work copy editing the manuscript.

The generous support I have received in Mexico humbles me. I thank the staff, librarians, and researchers of the Observatorio Urbano Local de la Ciudad de Cancún, the Universidad del Caribe, and the Universidad Autónoma de Yucatán. For helping me understand urban planning and housing policy and finance in Cancún, I thank Antorcha Campesina, CADU, CONDUSEF, Fundación Hogares, Grupo Sadasi, INFONAVIT, IMPLAN, INVIQROO, PROFECO, SEDUVI, and FONATUR, among others. I especially thank Andrés Aguilar Becerril, Luis Alam Fiasal, Ricardo Alvarado Guerrero, Edgar Campos García, Paulina Campos Villaseñor, Manuel Conde, Yeddelti Cupul Alonzo, Ana Rosa Duarte Duarte, Victor Ducoing Pedroza, Nélida Escobedo Ruiz, Juan Bosco García Galán, Rodolfo García Pliego, Jazmín Garnica Ortiz, Jorge Hammeken Arana, Alejandro Handall Díaz, Celina Izquierdo Sánchez, Ramón López Gual, Martín Martínez, Christine McCoy Cador, Pedro Moncada Jiménez, Liliana

Moreno Lucero, Federico Muñoz, José de Jesús Ramírez Fuentes, Regina Ruíz Gamboa, Jonathan Salazar Santos, David Sánchez Reyes, Bertha Valderrama Iturbe, Ariel Valtierra Hernández, Luis Alberto Velasco Ruiz, and Byrt Wammack Weber.

I have received incredible support during my time at the University of Minnesota. My colleagues and the staff in American Studies have provided me with a nurturing and stimulating environment. I have been enriched by my affiliation with the Department of American Indian Studies and the Department of Chicano and Latino Studies. My research assistants—Adriana González Neri, Tenzin Dhakong, Teodoro Crespo-Carrion, Elizabeth Ener, Vanessa Guzman, Isaac Lanan, Kerry McGuire, Kristina Perez, Kristina Silva Ara—were instrumental. This project could not have been completed without the generous funding provided by the Office of the Executive Vice President and Provost's Imagine Fund Faculty Award; the Global Programs and Strategy Alliance's Global Spotlight Faculty International Seed Grant; the Office of the Dean of the Graduate School's Grant-in-Aid of Research, Artistry and Scholarship; and the College of Liberal Arts Single Semester Leave Award and Sabbatical Leave and Sabbatical Supplement Award.

I believe we write in community. I thank my online writing group—Adriana Estill, Lourdes Gutiérrez Nájera, Desirée Martín, and Yolanda Padilla—for reading almost every word for the past four years. Your comments and *chisme* nurtured my writing and my soul. Lourdes deserves a special recognition for her honesty and brilliance, and for being my dearest friend and intellectual sounding board. Our conversations resonate throughout every page of this book. At the University of Minnesota, Christina Ewig, Lisa Hilbink, Elizabeth Friedman (as a visiting scholar), Lorena Muñoz, and Jessica Lopez Lyman inspire me on a daily basis to write creatively, persuasively, and fiercely. Your faith and friendship means a lot to me. For her unbelievable support beyond the book, I especially thank Jessica. Jennifer Pierce, Elliott Powell, and the graduate students in the American Studies Writing Group were great interlocutors. Pat Zavella always inspires me to think critically but keep my feet on the ground. I thank her for thoughtful review of the manuscript and for leading the charge with her exemplary work and activism. It has been a delight to collaborate with Matilde Córdoba Azcárate. I have learned so much from her profound insight on Yucatán. I thank Kevin Murphy for his generosity and for prompting me to engage with a settler colonial lens. Sharon Fischlowitz helped me see the centrality of the law in this project.

I thank the anonymous reviewers whose instructive comments greatly improved this book. For generously readings parts of this book, in some cases before it even was a book, I thank Anna Brailovsky, Kate Derrickson, Julia Elyachar, Donna Gabaccia, Karen Ho, Miranda Joseph, Megan McLean, and Bill Maurer. For engaging my ideas and making this a better project, I thank Arturo Aldama, Ryan Allen, Ragui Assaad, Drucilla Barker, Maylei Blackwell, Rachel Buff, Fernando Burga, Jeff Crump, Diane Davis, Monisha Das Gupta, Aaron Eddens, Kathy Fennelly, Vinay Gidwani, Edward Goetz, Jennifer Gunn, Georgia Hartman, Caroline Hervé, Shona Jackson, Toussaint Losier, Jasmine Mitchell, Paavo Monkkonen, Robert Nichols, Mario Obando, Karla Padrón, Lisa Park, David Pellow, Jeffrey Pilcher, Richard Rath, Alicia Re Cruz, Jan Rus, María Josefina Saldaña-Portillo, Shannon Speed, Rafael Tarrago, Michelle Téllez, and Mari Yoshihara. Jody Agius Vallejo, Lisa Martinez, Nitasha Sharma, Zulema Valdez, and Cara Wallis kept me accountable during different stages of this project. I participated in several reading groups that have left an imprint on this book. I thank the "Crisis Economics" Research Collaborative at the Institute for Advanced Study; the Mellon Sawyer seminar "The Politics of Land: Colony, Property, Ecology"; the "Gender and Capitalism" seminar in the Department of Gender, Women, & Sexuality Studies; the Grand Challenges Research Collaborative "Fostering Just and Equitable Societies and Assuring Clean Water and Sustainable Ecosystems"; and the Critical Latinx Indigeneities Working Group.

For inviting me to share my work, I thank the following people and institutions: Jessaca Leinaweaver and the Working Group on Anthropology and Population Colloquium at Brown University; Dylan Rodríguez and the Ethnic Studies Colloquium at University of California Riverside; Alicia Schmidt Camacho and the colloquium hosted by Ethnicity, Race, and Migration and Women, Gender, and Sexuality Studies at Yale University; Jacob Welch and the Yale Maya Lecture Series; Diane Davis and the "Risk and Resilience" Working Group of the Graduate School of Design at Harvard University; Samuel Jouault, Ana García de Fuentes, and Gustavo Marín Guardado and the Coloquio "Turismo, espacio y cultura" at the Universidad Autónoma de Yucatán; Paavo Monkkonen and the Latin American Cities Series at UCLA's Luskin School of Public Affairs; and Matilde Córdoba Azcárate and the Sawyer seminar "Claiming the City" at the International Institute at University of California San Diego; Ty Kāwika Tengan, Monisha Das Gupta, and the Ethnic Studies Colloquium at the University of Hawai'i at Manoa; and Georgia Hartman and Emilio de Antuñano and the "Housing

Across Borders" Symposium held at the Center for U.S.-Mexican Studies at UC San Diego. At the University of Minnesota, I received incisive feedback from the Department of Geography's GES Brown Bag; the "Gender and Capitalism" seminar; La Raza Student Cultural Center; the Office of International Programs' 2 Tuesday Global Spotlight Series; and the students in my graduate seminar "Indigenous Urbanism." As a resident fellow at the UMN's Institute for Advanced Study, I found a thriving community. The graduate students who participated in the "Risk and Resilience in Cancún, Mexico" workshop that I co-organized with Diane Davis for Harvard's Graduate School of Design research practicum prompted me to look at Cancún in new ways. I thank Seung Kyum Kim for permitting me to use his photographs.

I thank friends who reminded me to set aside the book to play, march, and advocate: Karen and Adam Aalgaard, Brittany Anderson, Raquel Arismendez, Irina Barrera, Alanna Barry, Dirk Binkley, Adriana Bravo Jones, Clint Carroll, Jack and Brook DeWaard, Heather and Brett Edelson, Theresa and Evran Ener, Kale Fajardo, Norma Garcés and the El Colegio High School Board, Britta Gauthier, Timothy "Cage" Hall, Walt Jacobs, Irene Lara, Angelica Lawson, Vanessa Litman, Joanna Núñez, Valerie Minor, Alberto Perez-Rendon, Jennifer Pierce, Tamara Ramirez, Rafael Solis Bravo, Gabriela Tsurutani, Rosy Vargas, and Dag Yngvesson.

Finally, in memoriam, I thank George Farrell, James A. Fox, and Eleuterio Po'ot Yah.

Indigenous Dispossession

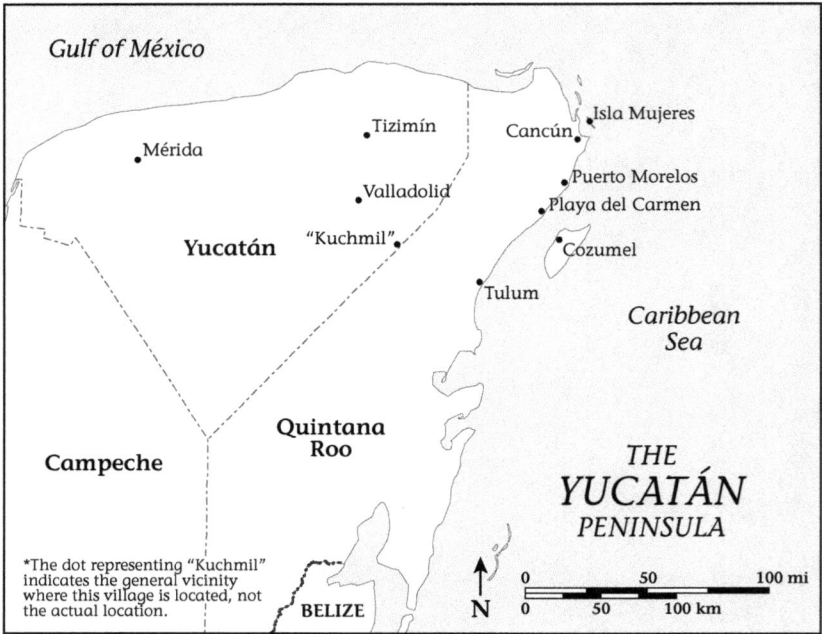

Gulf of México

Tizimín

Mérida

Cancún · Isla Mujeres

Valladolid

Puerto Morelos

Playa del Carmen

Yucatán · "Kuchmil"

Cózumel

Tulum

Caribbean
Sea

Quintana
Roo

Campeche

THE
YUCATÁN
PENINSULA

*The dot representing "Kuchmil" indicates the general vicinity where this village is located, not the actual location.

BELIZE

N

| 0 | 50 | 100 mi |
| 0 | 50 | 100 km |

MAP 1. The Yucatán Peninsula. Courtesy of Mike Foster of the University of Minnesota Cartography Lab.

Indigenous Cancún

TO PLAN A CITY into being is a formidable task of the imagination. In the mid-1960s, a group of Mexican bankers conceived the idea of building a city that would attract mass tourism to Mexico's Yucatán Peninsula. Cancún was considered first and foremost an economic investment. But constructing this international tourist center involved more than building infrastructure and recruiting settlers. It also entailed narrating a beginning and a future that made it possible to erase a past. *Cancun: Fantasy of Bankers*, the first history of Cancún, written by Mexican journalist Fernando Martí, captures these foundational fictions in the following description of Cancún:[1]

> [A] group of bankers conceived an absurd project: found a tourism city in dense jungle with the basic idea of capturing foreign exchange. The plan appeared to have neither head nor feet. As the site of their utopia, the bankers had chosen the Territory of Quintana Roo, geographically and logistically the furthest and most forbidding area in the nation, 2,000 kilometers from Mexico City and without a single international airport. The beaches selected were 200 kilometers from the nearest city, barely accessible by jeep paths snaking through swamps. Any reasonable observer could have confronted this group with a judicious question or two. Where, for example, were the half a million people needed to colonize the city going to come from in the little that remained of this century? That was the figure envisioned in the preliminary outline, but the document lacked a master colonization plan. The colonists would have to come voluntarily, arriving in the zone spontaneously. (1991, 7)

The bankers first propagated the fiction of an untouched "paradise," a tropical "utopia" (Martí 1991, 7, 18). In 1968, representing the Bank of Mexico, Antonio Enríquez Savignac and Ernesto Fernández Hurtado traveled Mexico's coastline until they arrived at Punta Cancún, in the Territory of Quintana Roo, proclaiming it "paradise itself" (quoted in Martí 1991, 18). This territory was considered an "abandoned frontier" and was not granted statehood until 1974 (Dachary 1998, 399). Attracted by the miles of coastline, the lack of development, and the positive results of state-led feasibility studies, Enríquez Savignac and Fernández Hurtado considered it perfect for tourist investment (Martí 1991, 18).[2] Enríquez Savignac, who later served as secretary of tourism under President Miguel de la Madrid (1982–88), explained, "Cancun [sic] is a Mexican development, conceived, planned, constructed and administered by Mexicans. This is important because it is the world's first tourism development from a base of zero . . . Cancun is a Mexican triumph" (quoted in Martí 1991, 9). Cancún was simultaneously imagined as terra nullius, a blank slate ready to be occupied, and as a tourist haven ready to be molded into a bustling city and an investment hub. By declaring themselves the masterminds behind this tourist "utopia" and economic success, Enríquez Savignac and Fernández Hurtado reinforced the fiction of a vacuous, undeveloped land.

Such an empty and geographically isolated space could only be civilized by the "spontaneous" arrival of half a million settlers (Martí 1991, 7). This narrative propagated the second fiction, of Cancún as a modern city made up of settlers. Unlike the colonial city of Mérida, which was built atop the thriving Maya ceremonial and sociopolitical center (kah) of Tihó, Cancún did not supplant a flourishing precolonial city.[3] The name Cancún was derived from the island of Cancun [sic], which would become permanently tethered to the mainland with the construction of the tourist center (see map).[4] The ceremonial centers of El Rey, San Miguel, Pok-ta-Pok, Punta Nizuc, Punta Ni'Kú, El Meco, and Koxolnah, located in and near Cancún, were not impressive or expansive enough to make them focal points for tourism (C. J. Walker 2009). Mexico's National Institute of Anthropology and History (Instituto Nacional de Antropología e Historia or INAH) did not begin excavating these ceremonial centers until after the city had been planned and hotel construction already begun (Con Uribe 2005).[5] As for the fishing community that predated the tourist center, it became a historical footnote to the founding of a modern metropolis. Architect Javier Solórzano drafted an urban plan to build a city, a hotel zone, and an airport. This plan neither acknowledged nor incorporated Maya fishermen and *campesinos* (peasants) who were recruited to form a veritable army of labor necessary to transform the landscape and to service tourists. Cancún's origin story hailed a future of a bustling metropole of settlers, tourists, and foreign dollars. As a result, Cancún's designation as a modern city severed its connection to a history of colonialism.

Cancún became a city without a past—the third fiction. The first posters advertising Cancún showcased empty beaches and tourists at play (Castellanos and Córdoba Azcárate, forthcoming). What is erased in this telling is the historical and contemporary presence of Maya people, the original inhabitants who prior to Spanish colonization built major urban centers like El Meco and who postconquest inhabit the towns and villages that dot the Yucatán Peninsula. In the few instances when Maya people are mentioned, they are depicted as transitory, as itinerant travelers. One popular poster stated: "This is Cancún. Where the Maya summered 1,000 years ago. Now you can live this world. CANCÚN. The new and millennial world of the Mexican Caribbean" (Martí 1991, 49). These words were imposed over the image of an empty, pristine beach, marred by a set of footprints, soon to be swept away by the incoming tide, reinforcing the narrative of a vanishing people. The preservation of the precolonial history of Cancún did not form part of the city's origin stories, although it has now been given a more prominent place with the 2012 opening of the Maya Museum (Museo Maya de Cancún).[6] Nor was Maya people's active resistance to predation under colonial and revolutionary governments acknowledged. In 1847, Maya rebels led one of the most successful Indigenous insurrections in the Americas, known as the Caste War, cementing this region's reputation in the popular imagination as "forbidding" and untamed (Reed 1964).[7] Tapped for their cheap labor and rich culture, Maya people played a foundational role in building and branding Cancún, which I discuss in detail in my book *A Return to Servitude* (2010a). Indigenous peoples currently make up one-third of Cancún's population.[8] Yet popular narratives of Cancún's origins—as a pristine "paradise," as a deserted island, as a "promised land," as "devoid of culture," as a "banker's fantasy," as a tourist site selected by a computer algorithm—consign Indigenous peoples to the past or efface them altogether.[9] Maya families residing in or near Punta Cancún at the time of Enríquez Savignac's visit, if mentioned at all, have been relegated to a few pages, while *ejidos* (communal landholdings) have been expunged from this history. Not surprisingly, Joaquín González Castro, mayor of Cancún from 1984 to 1987,

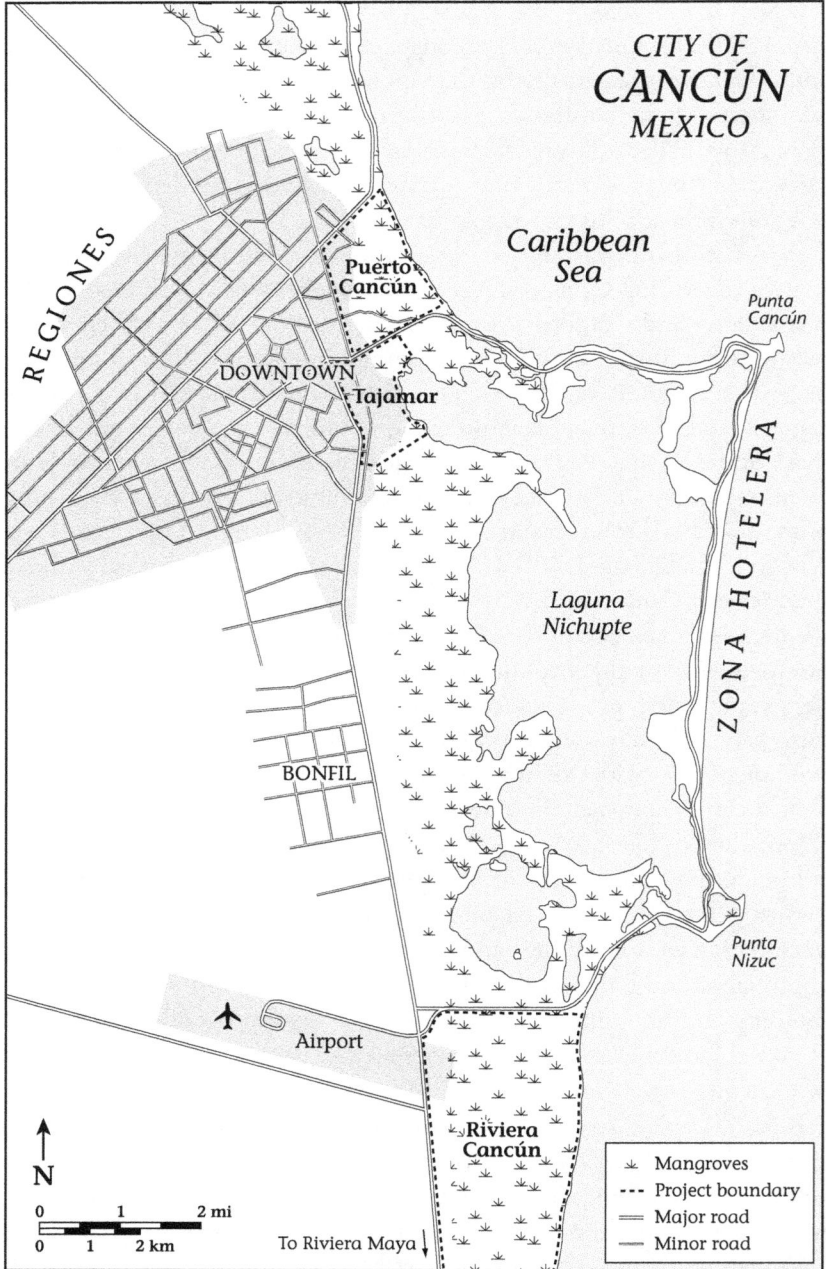

CITY OF
CANCÚN
MEXICO

Caribbean
Sea

Punta
Cancún

REGIONES

Puerto
Cancún

DOWNTOWN
Tajamar

ZONA HOTELERA

Laguna
Nichupte

BONFIL

Punta
Nizuc

Airport

N

| 0 | 1 | 2 mi |

| 0 | 1 | 2 km |

Riviera
Cancún

Mangroves
Project boundary
Major road
Minor road

To Riviera Maya

MAP 2. City of Cancún. Courtesy of Mike Foster of the University of Minnesota Cartography Lab.

described Cancún as "a mosaic and a laboratory. There are no natives here. We're all immigrants" (quoted in Martí 1991, 9). Rendering Cancún as *terra nullius* replete with vanishing Indians made it possible to reenvision Cancún as a modernist city. This strategy calls forth settler colonial logics of Indigenous elimination and displacement that aim to replace Indigenous peoples with settlers, logics that have dominated Anglophone imperial projects but have yet to be fully examined in Latin American colonialism.[10]

In this new technocratic social order, Indigenous histories are severed from modern urbanism and international finance. Historian Coll Thrush reminds us that urban centers are key sites of Indigenous dispossession and constitute the "grounds of settler colonialism" (2016, 15). Consigning Cancún to the status of modern metropolis occludes the colonial and settler colonial logics and technologies instrumental in shaping this city. Indeed, the myth of Cancún as a tropical utopia and investment "triumph" is a legacy of colonial and settler colonial projects.[11] The city of Cancún operates on the backs of Indigenous labor and is built upon land that was dispossessed from Indigenous people. In spite of these seizures, this land continues to form part of Indigenous collective traditions and historical memory. Placing the city outside of the nexus of relations—community, spatial, environmental, temporal, spiritual—masks the violent permutations of settler colonial discourse and governance (Dorries et al. 2019; Ramirez 2007a; Tang 2015). It also dismisses Indigenous peoples' active engagement with urban life, which has spurred a resurgence of intertribal identities and renewed efforts to demand urban land justice and claim rights to the city (Carpio 2011; Fixico 2000; Horn 2019; Lobo and Peters 2001; Negrín 2019). Centering the metropole as an Indigenous space reveals settler colonial policies and planning practices as racialized and discriminatory tactics that discipline and marginalize Indigenous peoples (Hugill 2019; Jackson, Porter, and Johnson 2018; Porter and Barry 2016; Walker, Jojola, and Natcher 2013).[12]

Heeding Thrush's call for a recovery of Indigenous histories as constitutive of the making of the metropole, this book begins by asserting Cancún as an Indigenous space. Acknowledging the entanglements of race and colonialism (in its varied manifestations) with modern urbanism calls attention to Indigenous urbanism as a crucial project of modern nation making and global capitalism. In highlighting Indigenous urbanism in relation to contemporary city spaces, I do not proclaim that urbanism is new, nor is it a singular experience for Indigenous peoples. Jack Forbes (2001) reminds us that Indigenous peoples have lived in urban centers since ancient times, as evidenced by the Maya city-states that dominated the Yucatán Peninsula prior to colonialism.[13] Maya peoples also have been highly mobile.[14] What is explored here is Indigenous people's relation to contemporary urbanism. In the case of cities built on Indigenous lands, as is the case with Cancún, we need to account for Indigenous place-making strategies and Indigenous belonging as integral parts of urbanism. United Nations Human Settlements Programme estimates that 87 percent of Latin America will be urban by 2050 (UN-Habitat 2012). Indigenous peoples form a key part of this urban migration. In Mexico, one-third of the Indigenous population lives in cities (Immigration and Refugee Board of Canada, 2008).

I rely on migration as a framework by which to capture the fluidity of Indigenous mobility across the Yucatán Peninsula. As Indigenous people move to cities, they may be positioned as settlers by the state and other institutions. Since my inquiry focuses on rural-urban migration within the peninsula, a region that is the traditional homeland of (Yucatec) Maya people, I do not frame Maya people as "settlers." Instead, I consider how Maya people engage these (re)positionings to demand rights to land and dignity. Indigenous peoples' understandings of space, territory, settlement, and environmental sustainability are increasingly being (un)settled by global economic recessions and neoliberal economic reforms throughout Latin America (Goodale and Postero 2013; Postero 2006; Sawyer 2004; Stephen 2013;).[15] Reframing the Latin American city through Indigenous experience follows the example of projects like *Detours* (Aikau and Vicuña Gonzalez 2019) that have produced decolonial guides to cityscapes that unearth the multilayered cultural geographies created by sovereign and autonomous Indigenous peoples and their diasporas.[16] These projects unsettle cities by disrupting the discovery narratives, imperial fantasies, and foundational fictions that have guided how we see and imagine Indigenous homelands. I aim to do similar work with the city of Cancún.

This book attends to contemporary Maya people's experiences with land and housing in Cancún. Specifically, it examines Indigenous home-ownership as an urbanizing experience that is intimately connected to a history of debt and dispossession and to new emerging financial markets. Since 2000, the Mexican government has promoted homeownership for its working poor, making "housing reform" a central component of its economic reforms.[17] Tract housing has become synonymous with economic development, generating a billion-dollar industry. The national push to move away from land reform and promote the tract house as symbolic of national belonging is transforming Indigenous peoples' relationship to land, urbanism, and finance. Through an ethnography of Maya migrants living in Cancún, one of Mexico's fastest growing cities, I examine how migrants make sense of the cultural, political, and legal ramifications of neoliberal housing policies that privilege mortgage finance over land redistribution. For Indigenous peoples, access to affordable housing is crucial to alleviating poverty. Yet Maya people have long associated debt with a history of debt peonage and land with freedom and autonomy. As *palapas* (traditional thatch and wood houses) are supplanted by thousands of tract houses, Maya migrants have learned to embrace debt and financial risk (fig. 1). I examine how this cultural shift and new aspirations transform Indigenous subjectivities, gender relations, and a tradition of collective landownership. How do these new aspirations overlap or come into conflict with market transitions and failures? How do Indigenous migrants withstand the racial and gender violence endemic to such transitions?

The central argument of this book is that as Indigenous migrants move to cities, they are no longer treated as Indigenous and instead become deracialized subjects who are disciplined through neoliberal instruments of debt, like mortgage finance and credit cards, leading to greater economic precarity and a loss of autonomy from the state. Maya migrants' struggles to

FIGURE 1. From *palapa* to tract housing. Photograph by author.

own a home reveal the colonial and settler colonial structures underpinning the city's economy, built environment, and racial order. As they grapple with predatory lending and foreclosure, Maya families cultivate strategies of resistance, from "waiting out" the state to demanding recognition as Indigenous people in urban centers. Through these maneuvers, Maya migrants forge a new vision of Indigenous urbanism that counters a discourse of urban malaise and articulates dignity with democracy.

In the Wake of Wilma and Other Calamities

Finding housing in Cancún has always been a challenge, especially as the half a million settlers became a reality. This book was driven by Maya migrants' preoccupation with finding *affordable* urban housing following the national shift away from land redistribution. Specifically, I focus on the period beginning in the year 2000 and concluding in January 2020, a couple of months prior to the COVID-19 pandemic. Migrants featured in this book come from the rural ejido of "Kuchmil," Yucatán. I use a pseudonym for this village and its residents to protect people's privacy and in deference to this community's valid concerns and fears over working with institutional actors, be they government officials or anthropologists.[18] In Kuchmil, land is valued as more than a commodity: it forms part of a moral economy that regulates social relations, protects sacred spaces, and fosters sustainable ecologies (Castellanos 2010b).[19] As prefabricated tract houses in social housing developments were marketed as an affordable option to the city's housing shortage, Maya migrants encountered a new property regime beset by a host of new bureaucracies and financial regulations, what I refer to as "housing reform." I began studying these reforms to help migrants negotiate Cancún's shifting land policies and real estate market, especially in the wake of Hurricane Wilma in 2005. The hurricane severely damaged homes that were built with recycled and traditional materials, like wood and thatch, prompting Maya families to question the durability of self-built homes. It's important to note that not all Maya families were willing to forgo procuring land to take on a mortgage. Many spoke critically of this system. By 2012, I was able to devote my time to investigating how Maya migrants were faring under housing reform, why some families were willing to take on debt, and why others were set against it. After that, I returned annually to conduct ethnographic research, but the bulk of the research was collected when I spent five months in Cancún in 2015. The book is based on over fifty interviews I conducted with Maya migrants, developers, mortgage lenders, government officials, activists, nonprofit organizations, and homeowners. I refer to public officials, mortgage lenders, and developers by name, unless they requested to remain anonymous. To understand the government's housing reform campaign, I analyze print media, including newspapers and advertisements. To understand Cancún's housing demographics and population dynamics, I analyze economic and census data.

Writing a book about how people manage their money and deal with financial crises takes trust. Before immigrating to the United States, my parents belonged to an ejido in the Mexican state of Colima. Listening to their stories and visiting with my aunts and uncles who remain members of the ejido instilled a respect for the land and the ejido. This fact helped establish my credibility as more than a mere *gringa* (foreigner) and anthropology student when I first arrived in Kuchmil in 1991. What began as an undergraduate research project under the guidance of anthropologists James Fox and Renato Rosaldo became a lifelong commitment to engage and collaborate with Kuchmil and its diaspora as its people endeavor to resist dispossession and maintain their autonomy. Over the years, this rapport has matured into deep and abiding friendships. Migrants were willing to speak frankly with me about their financial lives, personal dreams, and social commitments because of this longstanding collaboration and mutual regard. Nonetheless, I am cognizant of the imperial legacies and the power and privilege that continually shape these interactions.[20]

Migrants were careful to remind me that not all their stories were intended for public consumption. To protect my interlocutors' privacy and following Linda Tuhiwai Smith's decolonial approach to research (2012), I acknowledge and support Indigenous people's right to determine what information can be circulated to a wider audience. What I share here are the aspects of their lives Maya migrants are willing to make public. In exchange, Maya migrants asked me to serve as an intermediary as they navigated new systems of finance. They understood that, as a Western-based scholar with access to government officials and developers, I was positioned to get answers to their pending concerns over mortgage defaults and foreclosure and eviction proceedings. Instead of speaking on the behalf of Maya migrants, I organized workshops where migrants could pose their own questions about housing inequities. In conjunction with the Office of the Federal Attorney for the Consumer (Procuraduría Federal del Consumidor or PROFECO), I organized a financial literacy workshop on credit cards in January 2015. This was the first time PROFECO had held a workshop for Indigenous consumers in Cancún. I also worked with the National Commission for the Protection and Defense of Users of Financial Services (Comisión Nacional para la Protección y Defensa de los Usuarios de Servicios Financieros or CONDUSEF) to organize a workshop on foreclosures, but it was canceled after the state delegate unexpectedly stepped down from his position.

My aim to work in collaborative partnership with Indigenous communities is informed by Indigenous feminists' call for a decolonizing praxis that is territorially specific and challenges settler heteropatriarchy and settler capitalism (Arvin, Tuck, and Morrill 2013; Baldy 2018; J. Barker 2017; Green 2017; Ramirez 2007a; L. B. Simpson 2017; Smith 2012; Speed 2019). With a feminist psychologist, Dr. Liliana Moreno Lucero, I organized a gender workshop for Maya women who sought new tools for combating oppression against Indigenous women. As the leaders of land and housing struggles, Maya women face racial and gender violence. The two-day workshop created a space where Indigenous women shared stories and worked to heal from the trauma enacted by institutional racism, gender inequities, and state violence. I agreed not to circulate the intimate disclosures generated by this workshop, but I reference it here because we must be mindful of the ways race, class, and gender as interrelated systems of settler violence shape Indigenous women's lives and buttress the worlds of finance and urban planning.

My positionality as a Mexican-born feminist scholar trained in the United States has also deeply shaped this book. The questions I asked were grounded in a feminist praxis. Yet whom I could pose these questions to was delimited by my brown body and my privilege as a US academic. While Maya migrants generously agreed to talk with me about their experiences purchasing homes and land in Cancún because of my longstanding relationship with their community, I encountered many of the difficulties associated with "studying up" (Nader 1972). To understand the philosophies and promotional strategies of the administrators of mortgage banks and housing development agencies, I interviewed government administrators, land developers, and loan officers. Government administrators and land developers were willing to meet with me to talk about their "vision" for urban development in Cancún. The mortgage bank administrators and loan officers, in contrast, were evasive. I made numerous calls to set up appointments with the administrators of these private companies, only to be stood up or handed off to a lower-level administrator who could not answer my questions. I sat for hours in reception areas hoping to catch a word with administrators, but they were always too busy or had "too much work." What I share here is a partial accounting of Indigenous land and housing struggles, but one that I hope will generate a greater investment in understanding Indigenous urbanisms.

Indigenous Dispossession

This book is a deliberation on Indigenous dispossession. Indigeneity is a relational and historical category deployed by governments and capital to justify dispossession, produce difference, and solidify empires (Byrd 2011; O'Brien 2010; Vimalassery, Hu Pegues, and Goldstein 2016). This approach acknowledges that colonialism is not a monolithic project but comprises ideological and historical formations shaped by social, racial, and economic structures (Mignolo 2005; Quijano 2000; Wolfe 1999). By displacing Indigenous peoples and in some places eliminating them altogether, colonialism(s) became space-making projects that transformed geographic and social landscapes through acts of violence, genocide, and terror (Saldaña-Portillo 2016). In the process, indigeneity—that is, the cultural, political, and racial representations of being Indigenous—became a marker to construct difference by distinguishing settlers from Indigenous peoples and by creating the categories of the *indio* (Indian), *mestizo* (mixed race Indian and Spaniard) and *criollo/creole* (a person born in the Americas) (e.g., Jackson 2012).[21] These distinctions asserted and reinforced power differentials that determined who could own land and who received the benefits of full citizenship.

The shift from colonialism to nationalism did not conclude this history of radical alterity and dispossession. Inspired by liberal ideologies of equality and political sovereignty, independence from Spain has been immortalized in Latin America as a move from colonial subjugation to liberation. As the colonial systems regulating Indigenous lives were dismantled (like *repartimiento* and *encomiendas*), Indigenous communities faced new strategies of containment and elimination.[22] Land usurpation became central to nationbuilding projects and remains so under neoliberal regimes. In contemporary Mexico, state efforts to promote property rights and homeownership are tied to a long history of dispossession. To draw out these connections, I apply Indigenous dispossession as a framework that articulates the *longue durée* of colonial and settler colonial projects with Indigenous people's contemporary experiences with land loss under neoliberal regimes. Analyses of contemporary Indigenous dispossession have been understood primarily through a political and legal framework.[23] In her study of Indigenous women in US detention centers, for example, Shannon Speed (2019) demonstrates how the neoliberal settler state continues to rely on tactics of elimination and dispossession. Other studies highlight the active role of Indigenous peoples in theorizing dispossession.[24] For example, Jodi Byrd reminds us that "Indigenous peoples must be central to any theorization of the conditions of postcoloniality, empire, and death-dealing regimes that arise out of Indigenous lands" (2011, xiv). This book focuses primarily on Indigenous people's understanding of and engagement with dispossession in urban settings. It considers how Indigenous conceptions of home and property draw upon historical memory to produce a situated understanding of loss and autonomy in an era of increasing urbanization and financialization.

This book maps out the convergence of colonial and settler colonial projects to examine Indigenous dispossession in Mexico, and thus extends my previous analysis on settler colonialism in Latin America in *American Quarterly* (2017). Settler colonialism is a form of colonialism that is predicated on Indigenous dispossession and elimination (Wolfe 1999). Primarily associated with the Anglophone world, settler colonialism has rarely been discussed in relation to Latin America.[25] Instead, regimes of colonialism in the Americas were distinguished by their method of dispossession, as rooted in *either* land or labor expropriation: US settler colonialism was premised on land extraction, Indigenous elimination, and settler occupation, whereas colonialism in Latin America was based on the extraction of Indigenous labor. This paradigm prompted a reluctance to apply a settler colonial framework to Latin America (Sánchez and Pita 2014; Saldaña-Portillo 2016). Recent works questioning this paradigm, conducted by myself, Juan Castro, Richard Gott, Lourdes Gutiérrez Nájera, Korinta Maldonado, Baron Pineda, Manuela Picq, Ricardo Salvatorre, and Shannon Speed, have identified a multiplicity of settler colonial projects throughout the Americas. I apply this paradigm to urban Latin America.

In Mexico, the logic of dispossession is manifested in *both* land and labor extraction, thus offering an example that blurs the land/labor distinction used to distinguish colonialism in the Americas.[26] During the colonial period, the *encomienda* system of tribute displaced Indigenous peoples by forcing them to resettle in larger towns. Abolished by royal decree in 1718, the demise of the *encomienda* paved the way for the rise of the hacienda system, where Indigenous peasants participated in contract labor as *peones* (workers).[27] After Mexican independence from Spain in 1810, liberal politics led to increasing land alienation. The rights and protection granted to Indian *pueblos* by the Catholic Church and the colonial government were no longer upheld by the Mexican government, spurring land encroachment. Similar processes of land dispossession took place throughout Latin America (Castro and Picq 2017; Di Giminiani 2018). The postrevolutionary Mexican government aimed to redress these land disputes through a policy of land redistribution through the fortification of the ejido system (Eisenstadt 2011). But this process also entailed promoting non-Indigenous settlement on Indigenous lands located in conflict-ridden regions. For example, the Echeverría administration (1970–76) provided peasants from states like Michoacán and Tabasco with grants to land deemed "uncolonized" in the states of Quintana Roo and Chiapas (Collier 1994, 43; Schmidt 1991).[28]

Despite postrevolutionary efforts to curb land encroachment, the process of land extraction and Indigenous elimination through assimilation sped up under neoliberal regimes, undergirded by liberal ideas of creating a democracy based on property ownership. Land redistribution programs ended with the 1994 North American Free Trade Agreement (NAFTA), paving the way for the privatization of ejido lands by making it permissible for *ejidatarios* (members of the ejido) to sell, rent, sharecrop, or mortgage land parcels to foreign capital. The primary outcome of land reform after NAFTA was to displace Indigenous peoples from their lands, making them readily available as surplus labor. Given that ejido lands made up over half of Mexico's cultivable land, NAFTA's impact has been compared to the English Enclosure Movement and the United States' 1887 Dawes General Allotment Act ("Reform of Article 27" 1994). The English Enclosure Acts, which were enacted in the 1700s through the 1800s, divided communal lands into individually owned farms, while the Dawes Act divided Indian tribal lands and made them available for public sale to white settlers. NAFTA took place centuries after these acts, but its push to privatize communal lands held in trust by Indigenous communities situates it within the tragedy of the commons.

David Chang astutely notes that new policies of enclosure "simultaneously extended and masked the reach of state power" (2011, 109). Neoliberal regimes are more than just echoes of earlier colonial projects. They are based on models of extraction, but they also comprise projects of elimination. As such, they are being reinterpreted as a new iteration of settler colonialism (Speed 2017, 2019; Castro and Picq 2017; Loperena 2017). Settler colonial theory offers a new lens by which to think through the ramifications of settler colonial tactics in Latin America. Settler colonial logics are considered to originate in US empire, but they have also been deployed in Latin America, especially under neoliberal regimes. Tracing the "technologies of settler belonging and their ability to be refashioned and redeployed" in Mexico, I connect ejido dispossession with neoliberal policies of urban land development and expanding real estate markets (Jackson 2012, 60). This approach helps us examine the colonial and settler colonial logics that have transformed an Indigenous landscape into the settler colony of Cancún.

When I first visited Cancún, I arrived as a tourist, but one who had spent a summer conducting an ethnographic project in Kuchmil. I was guided by tour books that peddled the fiction of a city with an ancient past and of an untouched paradise converted into a booming tourist center by Mexican technocrats. Yet my experience living in Kuchmil and spending time with Kuchmil migrants in Cancún prompted me to question the veracity of these narratives. Cancún's architecture and hotel zone may be construed as "modern," but Kuchmil migrants reminded me that Cancún formed part of a sacred geography and was embedded in longstanding struggles for Indigenous autonomy. To understand Cancún, it is necessary to delve into this history.

In colonial Yucatán, land was concentrated in the hands of the church, Indigenous *pueblos*, and colonists who benefitted from the *encomienda* system. During nationalism, Indigenous communal lands in Yucatán, which consisted of uncultivated forests, were appropriated by private owners for use in the commercial agricultural production of henequen, sugar, corn, and cotton on haciendas (Joseph 1988; Rugeley 1996). The shift in mode of production from subsistence to commercial agriculture reduced the amount of land available to Maya peasants, forcing independent subsistence farmers to become *peones* on haciendas. Maya concerns over land incursions and heavy taxation prompted rebellions and led to the Caste War of 1847, a fifty-year battle that took place in southeastern Yucatán (Redfield 1941; Reed 1964; Rugeley 1996). The war prompted Spanish settlers to flee the region and compelled Maya peasants to take up arms or hide in the jungle, thereby designating southeastern Yucatán as dangerous and abandoned. The creation of the Territory of Quintana Roo by the Díaz administration (1877–80, 1884–1911) in 1902 was intended to quell offshoots of this insurrection and to repopulate the region.

The lives of Maya migrants from my study reflect this history of Indigenous dispossession in Yucatán. Migrants' desire for land originated from their families' history of peonage on haciendas and their own participation in the ejido system. Their great grandparents worked as *peones* on haciendas located in southeastern Yucatán, a practice locally referred to as *esclavitud* (slavery). With the onset of the Caste War in this region, they escaped the haciendas and debt peonage and participated in the war as devotees of the speaking cross, known as the *Santa Cruz*, which rallied Maya rebels to keep fighting (see Reed 1997). In spite of the turmoil triggered by war and debt peonage, these families did not stray far from the *tuuch* (belly button) in Xocen, one of six sacred and ancient shrine centers that make up a sacred geography and connect patronymic clan lineages (Sullivan 1989). In the late 1890s, as they searched for the ideal place to make *milpa* (corn), they opted to settle on a postclassic Maya site, which they named "Kuchmil," which was tied to their patronymic clan lineages and was surrounded by dense forest with access to fresh water from an ancient well. The community soon benefited from the Mexican government's efforts to redress land disputes in response to revolutionary mandates. From 1915 to 1933, one-fifth of land in the state of Yucatán was decreed ejido land, formally recognizing peasants' rights to work it (Brannon 1991). In 1931, Kuchmil was included in an ejido grant that encompassed three other pueblos. Ejido land was held in common and organized collectively on a rotation system. As a result of these experiences, land for Maya communities came to represent a sacred geography, a primary source of food, freedom from slavery, and autonomy from the state (Castellanos 2010b; Eiss 2002, 2010; Re Cruz 1996a; Sullivan 1989; Villa Rojas 1978). Not surprisingly, Maya migrants attach many of these meanings to land in Cancún. Land represents more than private property as recognized by the state. Cancún is situated on land that forms part of a sacred geography for Maya peoples and that provides essential resources for the maintenance of Indigenous practices. Land is also a symbol of freedom from tourism and the state, regardless of the significant role the state has played in providing migrants with access to land.

Yet obtaining land in Cancún is extremely difficult, especially as land once again has become increasingly concentrated in private hands. Cancún's 1974 master plan failed to include housing for the working class, thereby limiting how migrants could obtain land and/or a house. Prior to housing reform, migrants procured land in the following ways. One option was for migrants to purchase land on the private market. Since affordable plots rarely went up for sale, few migrants could rely on this approach. The second option involved squatting on ejido land or land that was deemed "unoccupied," regardless of ownership. This was a popular tactic in the early days of Cancún's history (McLean n.d.), but opportunities for squatting dwindled with the city's expansion as the state and developers snapped up large tracts of land. The third option entailed petitioning the state for a land allotment. Although it meant long waiting periods, this was the most popular and affordable option for self-help housing. As the Mexican government began pivoting away from land redistribution in 2000, its land reserves dwindled, and it began to phase out government-subsidized land allotments, making it increasingly difficult for Maya migrants to obtain land. This divestment has increased urbanization (Vásquez Castillo 2004). The fourth option was to purchase a house with the aid of government programs. However, few migrants earned sufficient income to qualify for these programs. Social housing was proposed as an affordable solution, leading to the construction of thousands of hectares of tract housing in Cancún.

To own a home today, Maya migrants must learn to embrace debt on a scale previously unimaginable and unattainable. The private developer has become the modern day *hacendado*, especially in urban centers like Cancún, where ejido land has been commodified and homes can be converted into debt. The rise in homeownership among the lower middle and working classes in Cancún stimulated greater access to formal credit from banks, microfinance lenders, and retail stores. Mortgage debt—and the accompanying credit opportunities it made possible—binds migrants to Cancún's shifting economic future as a settler colony and urban metropole. Maya migrants' forays with a new credit economy can be attributed as an outcome of modernization and to the Mexican government's efforts to integrate Indigenous peoples into national economies. However, this interpretation ignores the ways shifting land tenure practices spanning colonial and settler colonial periods have led to Indigenous dispossession and circumscribed Indigenous autonomy within urban spaces and under neoliberal regimes.

Indigenous Urbanism(s) in Latin America

Cancún has long been considered a tourist mecca, but its role as an urban metropole has been overlooked. As a modern city celebrating its fiftieth anniversary in 2020, Cancún forms part of a history of modernist projects begun in the early twentieth century with the intent to radically transform urban life in Latin America (García de Fuentes 1979; McCoy Cador 2017; McCoy Cador and Hernández von Wobeser 2020). Cities like Brasilia, as James Holston (1989) shows, were premised on a New World mythology of colonization and a narrative of progress severed from the past, including previous failures of development. These analyses acknowledge the colonial fictions upon which the modern city was built and the pre-Columbian influences undergirding these utopias (Bergdoll et al. 2015; Fraser 2001; O'Rourke 2017). However, these studies do not consider the role Indigenous people played in building the city as is the case in Cancún. Nor do they consider how Indigenous people have inhabited the modern city and reshaped utopic visions and the built environment by their very presence and through practices such as squatting and selling ejido parcels for development. In Bolivia and Ecuador, Philipp Horn (2019) shows that Indigenous peoples are actively engaged with demanding rights to the city and creating more inclusive urban spaces. Despite these demands, the modern city is racialized as mestizo, not Indigenous, masking the ties between the colonial, settler colonial, and urban histories that have led to Indigenous dispossession in the metropole. Recent efforts to decolonize urban planning attest to the urgency of this inquiry (Harjo 2019; Jackson et al. 2018; Walker et al. 2013). In her study of Wixarika rights to the cities of Guadalajara and Tepic, Diana Negrín (2019) stresses that attending to the distinctive historical and geographic experiences of Indigenous peoples in urban spaces is a crucial step in dismantling racial difference in contemporary Mexico.

Studies of contemporary urbanism make a similar assumption. Urbanism continues to be framed primarily as a mestizo experience. Indigenous people may inhabit the city, but their experiences do not figure prominently in urban theory. Instead, these studies frame the Latin American city as a struggle between development that is planned (e.g., modernist projects) and unplanned (e.g., shantytowns). Recent approaches to urban informality have challenged this binary by underscoring the entangled and dependent relationship between the formal and the informal (Fischer, McCann and Auyero 2014; Kusno 2013; Roy and AlSayyad 2004; Simone 2004). Indeed, Latin American cities have come to be defined as much by their formal urbanity as their informal development. For example, impoverished shantytowns have come to epitomize informality in the popular imagination, but their growth cannot be disentangled from the formal structures of urban planning, land ordinances, and municipal governance. Where, when, and why shantytowns emerge can tell us much about the politics of land development in an urban metropolis. Yet what is missing from this debate is how race and indigeneity gets mapped onto land politics and urban planning.[29] Despite efforts to move beyond the informal/formal dichotomy, this binary deserves attention because it alludes to other divides—rural/urban, Indigenous/settler, colonial/modern—that constitute the foundational fictions that animate the history of Cancún and that are based on progressive narratives of development premised on a savage/civilized continuum. In Cancún, the informal has come to be equated with squatters and with shantytowns that supplant ejido land and tropical forest. What is deemed informal then is closely aligned with the narrative of *terra nullius* and its accompanying mantra of "there are no natives here, only settlers," including Maya people who are positioned as "settlers." The city's slogan "Orgullosamente cancunense y dignamente quintanarroense" (Proudly of Cancún and honorably of Quintana Roo) showcases how urban identity hinges on a deracialized citizenship that is embraced even by some Maya migrants. This narrative reinforces the absence of an Indigenous presence in urban spaces. Similarly, treatises on the modern city associate poverty and marginality with informality but not with indigeneity (see Fischer et al. 2014; Perlman 2010; Roy and AlSayyad 2004).

The estrangement between urban studies and Indigenous histories is a residue of imperial legacies that consign Indians to rural spaces (Thrush 2016). Indigenous peoples have long been associated with the rural and peasant resistance in Latin America (Assies 2008; Baitenmann 1997, 1998, 2005; Barnes 2009; Cornelius and Myhre 1998; Gledhill 1995; Léonard and Losch 2009; Nuijten 2003; Purnell 1999; Warman 1980, 1985). Yet in the case of Mexico, a third of its Indigenous population is primarily concentrated in urban centers, the majority of whom reside in shantytowns, where land rights are contested or in flux. I conceive of "Indigenous urbanism" as a way to rethink the city and its foundational fictions by engaging with the binaries of rural/urban, mestizo/*indio*, and formal/informal and their entangled histories. It does so by foregrounding relations, reciprocity, and the specificity of place.[30] As such, Indigenous urbanism(s) constitute key features of urban development in Cancún. This approach builds on scholars like Guillermo Bonfil Batalla (1996), Andrew Canessa (2012), Charles Hale (2006), Alcida Ramos (1998), and Mary Weismantel (2001), who illuminate the racial hierarchies and racial ambivalences that structure and define indigeneity in Latin America.

Studies of Indigenous peoples in Latin America tend to situate these communities in relation to social and environmental movements aimed at combating neoliberal policies and extractivism (Eisenstadt 2011; Loperena 2017; Lucero 2008; Speed 2008). The resurgence in Indigenous organizing and activism, however, has not led to a reduction in inequality, nor to greater recognition and respect for Indigenous communities, as demonstrated by the recent works of Sarah Radcliffe, Nancy Postero, and Matilde Córdoba Azcárate. Developmental practices, Sarah Radcliffe (2015) shows, retain colonial associations of difference that reinforce inequality and thus offer limited gains for rural Indigenous women, even when they are the principal targets for these policies. Similarly, Nancy Postero (2017) argues that decolonizing efforts by the "Indigenous state" have not produced an emancipatory politics but instead have solidified the state's reliance on market capitalism, further exacerbating inequality. Tourism economies, Matilde Córdoba Azcárate (2020) points out, are based on extractivist and predatory logics that have dire consequences for the communities that live with tourism and for the ecologies in which tourism is embedded. She suggests that Indigenous peoples become stuck with tourism and are grateful for it, even as they condemn the logics that bind them to it. This book draws from these critiques of neoliberalism but diverges from these analyses by focusing on Indigenous experiences with urban housing, an area of inquiry that has yet to be examined in depth in Latin America. It attends to the ways urban planning and housing and credit markets reproduce deracialized subjects and make Indigenous peoples invisible in the metropole. Housing reform becomes a form of discipline to produce new types of citizens through narratives that bind personal responsibility, private property, and debt, and eschew collective ownership, solidarity, and Indigenous rights.

From Nations in Debt to Individual Debtors

Financialization is not just a process of economic restructuring. It becomes an embodied, situated, and lived experience deeply influenced by history and racial, class, and gender systems, according to recent scholarship (D. K. Barker and Feiner 2004; Bourdieu 2005; Cattelino 2008; Chu 2010; Desmond 2016; Elyachar 2002; Ho 2009; M. Joseph 2014; Zelizer 2010). Concepts like risk, credit, and debt are social formations that reflect and construct moral and cultural orders based on notions of liberal individualism, progressive evolutionism, and moral economies (Beck 2008; Douglas and Wildavsky 1983; Graeber 2011; Guseva 2008; Levy 2012; B. Williams 2004). The 2008 US mortgage crash offers an example of the collapse and reconstitution of this moral order and thus provides a frame of reference for thinking through financialization in other contexts.[31] Economic crises and restructuring call attention to the constructed nature of economics, of how categories, measurements, and practices not only change over time, but how they can become disembedded or even hijacked from their original intent to promote or defend new ways of managing populations and creating new social orders.

In Latin America, research on economic restructuring is concentrated on the moment that created nations in debt in the Global South and the impact of current neoliberal reforms. Debt crises began in the 1970s as Latin American countries borrowed heavily and then were unable to pay back their debt (Auerbach 2001; D. Gilbert 2007; Nash 2006). Austerity measures, imposed to restructure this debt during the 1980s and 1990s, privatized state-owned enterprises, deregulated economic policies, and reduced social spending (Nash 2006; Sawyer 2004). Studies have shown how the dismantling of the welfare state and the elimination of subsidies displaced these costs onto the backs of the working poor, who absorbed cuts in childcare, food subsidies, employment, and benefits. Although neoliberal reforms have led to state retrenchment, the state continues to deeply influence everyday practices and collective action (Auyero 2012; Bourdieu 2005; Ellison 2018; Gupta 1995, 2012; G. Joseph and Nugent 1994; Miller and Rose 2013; Scott 1998, 2010). At the same time, new governing coalitions rallied for social policies, based on a market model of privatization, to reform labor laws, social security, and banking systems (Cortes 2009; Grugel and Riggirozzi 2009). These reforms begat greater inequality between the rich and the poor (Babb 2001, 2011; Dávila 2012; Goodale and Postero 2013; Hellman 1995; Otero 1996; L. Walker 2013). The current push to promote consumer debt, microfinance, and real estate markets is creating a nation of *individual* debtors in the Global South (James 2015; Rus and Rus 2014; Stoll 2013).

There are social and moral implications of the current push to produce nations of individual debtors (James 2015; Karim 2011; Rus and Rus 2014; Soederberg 2014; Stoll 2013). Examining how Indigenous peoples engage with changing financial systems, especially during moments of economic crises, reveals the ways in which marginalized and impoverished Indigenous communities experience neoliberal policies and development in their daily lives. Indigenous communities are deeply aware that the individualizing of debt and the financialization of life have historically been strategies for Indigenous dispossession. This book looks at Indigenous people's invocations of community and reciprocity to challenge and resist debt.

Housing with Dignity

Housing offers a prime opportunity to evaluate indebtedness. In the wake of the 2008 global real estate collapse, housing becomes a contested site for the intergenerational politics of gender, domesticity, and citizenship.[32] Susan Lobo (1982) and Edward Murphy (2015) show that notions of propriety, domesticity, and personhood go hand in hand in historically shaping housing policies and individual aspirations for homeownership in Peru and Chile. As land becomes increasingly privatized thus curtailing a tradition of self-help housing, access to housing will become limited to tract housing. In countries with robust housing programs like Mexico, Brazil, and Chile, the growth in this type of homeownership is increasingly attributed to low- and moderate-income families (Bredenoord, van Lindert, and Smets 2014; Jha 2007). This transition calls attention to the ways housing destabilizes and reconfigures migrant lives, even as it aims for stability and security, and creates new entanglements of ideologies of home, self, and state (Carsten 2004; Han 2012; Leinaweaver 2009; Sandoval-Cervantes 2017). The housing crash makes it possible to apprehend mortgage debt as constructing new forms of subjectivities that emerge through the conjuncture of lived experience and market rationalities (Mbembe and Roitman 1995). In her study of the 2008 US housing crash in California's Sacramento Valley, Noelle Stout (2019) exposes the ties of mutuality and reciprocity that bind borrowers and lenders. When banks foreclosed on homes, they severed these social ties, leading some homeowners to walk away or refuse to pay their debt. In Mexico, lived experience is overlooked by studies that focus on housing policy in major metropolitan regions and its relationship with the poverty industry. These macrostudies show that housing reform is leading toward greater residential and socioeconomic segregation and insecurity and has become a disciplinary tactic that convinces surplus laborers to go into debt by participating in microfinance lending (Monkkonen 2012; Soederberg 2014; Ward, Jiménez Huerta, and Di Virgilio 2015). If we consider debt to be productive, relational, and asymmetrical (Mauss 1967; Roitman 2003), then what kinds of dependencies, anxieties, and subjectivities does it produce among Indigenous homeowners? As Deborah James (2015) has shown for South Africa, relying on debt to enable national and middle-class aspirations can lead to greater precarity. How migrants live with economic precarity after housing reform can illuminate how global finance, residential segregation, and tourism produce new urban subjects and spatialize risk and debt across generations.

For the Mexican government, Mexico's future success is largely associated with becoming a "property-owning democracy" (De Soto 2000; "Housing in Mexico" 2004). Since the 1960s, housing policy in Mexico has evolved to accommodate immense population growth and urbanization, with federal housing construction initially benefiting the middle class.[33] Much of the country's urban growth has been propelled by self-help housing (Bredenoord and Cabrera Montiel 2014; Ward 1990, 1998), with 40 percent of Mexicans lacking what the government calls "dignified" or "adequate" housing (Elias and Ritchie 2008); that is, housing built according to national safety standards, resistant to natural disasters, that provides access to basic services (electricity, potable water, and sewage disposal), and includes legal rights to property as decreed by the Federal Housing Law.[34] This housing deficit is seen both as a problem for Mexico's transformation into a modern nation and as an economic opportunity to expand a thriving real estate market. The shift to promote social housing is connected to Mexico's history of economic crises, followed by periods of deregulation as economic reform. The 1994 peso and bank crises caused inflation rates on home loans to skyrocket. As banks put in place strict requirements for credit approval, the number of mortgages and credit available was drastically reduced, excluding much of Mexico's working class and a large sector of its middle class. Access to housing was further restricted by the 1992 Agrarian Law, which promoted the privatization of ejido land and ended state administered land redistribution. As a result, millions of poor and working-class Mexicans in need of housing could no longer petition the state for land.

To solve the housing deficit, President Vicente Fox's administration (2000–2006) restructured Mexico's real estate market to attract foreign investment and to provide affordable housing for its working poor. These reforms included liberalizing the federal housing program to permit previously ineligible working-class families to qualify for mortgages, introducing cofinancing programs, and subsidizing private capital to increase the construction of affordable housing units for the working poor. Social housing and lending, advocated by financial institutions and development agencies like the World Bank and subsidized by the Mexican state, has targeted working-class migrants. The government also expanded the number of loans made available through public agencies like the National Institute for Funding Workers' Housing (Instituto del Fondo Nacional de la Vivienda para Trabajadores or INFONAVIT). Established in 1972, the government-run INFONAVIT provides low-interest mortgages to Mexicans employed in the formal sector and allows them to save toward a down payment through a fund that requires employers to contribute 5 percent of an employee's daily wage. In 2005, INFONAVIT relaxed its rules to include informal wages in income tallies and to permit joint financing with mortgage lenders, thus making social housing affordable to the working and lower middle classes.

President Enrique Peña Nieto's 2013 National Housing Policy (Política Nacional de Vivienda) expanded these measures to foster institutional coordination and promote sustainable urban development. INFONAVIT loans soon made up over half of all mortgage loans in Mexico (UN-Habitat 2011). By 2017, former INFONAVIT Director Sebastián Fernández Cortina proclaimed that 70 percent of all home loans were provided by INFONAVIT.[35] Mexico's housing reform is being promoted throughout Latin America by organizations like the World Bank as a model for sustainable and affordable housing (Jha 2007; Stickney 2014). Even newly elected President Andrés Manuel López Obrador, who has implemented bureaucratic cuts, continues to support INFONAVIT and has prescribed reforms to expand and solidify its scope nationwide.[36]

But how effective are these policies? Recent concerns over delinquency rates among homeowners and rising insecurity associated with abandoned housing point to the risks involved in promoting these reforms. While critiques highlight the social isolation and segregation that plague Mexico's new housing developments (Inclán-Valadez 2013, 2014; Monkkonen 2012; Reyes Ruiz del Cueto 2013), few studies focus on Indigenous residents' lived experience with financial processes and housing inequities. A comprehensive study of INFONAVIT social housing in seven Mexican cities identified key challenges and called for localized approaches for redensification and sustainable development (Davis 2016). This book addresses these challenges through an account of Indigenous urbanism.

Overview

Indigenous migrants' forays into urban real estate markets offer a prime opportunity to evaluate how they embrace and challenge racialized and gendered discourses of progress and modernity. Studying the new aspirations of Indigenous migrants and the national and cultural shift toward individual homeownership, including its association with speculative accumulation, offers a frame for understanding the transformation of Indigenous subjectivities, gender relations, and a tradition of collective landownership. Analyzing Indigenous people's engagement with new forms of debt and risk illuminates shifts in moral frameworks previously based on collapsing the past, present, and future. I argue that in their quest for "dignified" housing, Maya migrants have become more reliant on the market for economic security, which in turn has led to greater economic insecurity under current economic conditions and has prompted levels of indebtedness and dispossession not seen since the nineteenth century. As real estate markets continue to expand in Latin America, how Maya migrants negotiate new forms of dispossession and speculation, especially in an urban context, will have lasting political and policy implications.

Chapter 1 maps out the history of land policies in Cancún and how they have been shaped by ideologies of family, gender, and citizenship. By focusing on Maya migrants' experiences with housing, this chapter draws attention to how these ideologies intersect with Indigenous struggles for autonomy. Chapter 2 examines the Fox administration's campaign promoting "dignified" housing. Analyzing news articles and housing policies, I trace the ideological discourses undergirding the national shift away from land redistribution. Through a focus on one Maya family's decision to purchase a home in a social housing development, this chapter shows how the language of patrimony and suburban domesticity is used to align individualized debt with national ideals.

Chapter 3 analyzes Indigenous migrants' willingness to take on debt. Prior to 2000, Maya migrants aspired to own property, but without debt. Homeownership has increased Maya migrants access to credit, making them the "new frontier" of capitalism. But it has concomitantly increased their economic risk. As Maya migrants embrace debt to purchase goods and homes, I examine how credit and risk take on a gendered and "moral valence" (Zavisca 2012, 7). For male migrants, taking on a mortgage is a risky venture that harks back to Indigenous experiences with debt peonage. Yet for female migrants, owning a prefabricated home represents progress *and* security. To tease out this moral, cultural, and gendered dilemma, I examine migrants' exposure to microfinance and credit cards.

Chapter 4 examines a Maya family's experience with foreclosure. I delve into the anger and pain evoked during this moment of crisis and its association with a history of Indigenous dispossession in Mexico. How do Indigenous people cope with this loss, and how does it (re)structure their attachments to place, land, and nation? Even as housing reform becomes a form of discipline and constructs new narratives of progress, debt delinquency, and insecurity, I show how migrants' resistance strategies, from foot dragging to legal suits to postponing foreclosure, are transformed into a process of "waiting out" the state and capital. By "waiting out" INFONAVIT and the mortgage company, Maya migrants sidestep the bureaucratic measures created to regulate the poor and convert consent into provocative acts of obstruction and defiance.

Chapter 5 examines the case of Maya migrants who reject social housing and instead opt to live in the squatter settlement of Colonia Mario Villanueva. This chapter follows the *colonia*'s legal battle to avoid eviction. Social housing, Maya migrants argue, entails great risk (due to mortgage debt) and is rife with social atomization and violence. In contrast, life in Colonia Mario Villanueva is organized around principles of solidarity that invoke Indigenous communal land practices. This struggle to postpone eviction was led by Maya women, who relied on strategies of resistance derived from Indigenous land struggles. *Colonias* are perfect places to cultivate political subordination, but in the case of Mario Villanueva, they also become spaces of insubordination.

The book concludes by assessing how Indigenous migrants have fared under housing reform. What does it mean to be Indigenous and in debt today? Although urban development in Cancún has taken on a US model of suburbanization, it has been supported by a different set of financial mechanisms, in this case significant government subsidies for developers, mortgage lenders, and homeowners. Maya migrants have long equated tourist work with debt peonage. Now, as they face pernicious forms of debt, how is this cautionary tale being reworked to explain their current economic woes and moral dilemmas? Migrants have moved away from previous desires for autonomy from the state to become reliant on themselves and the market, making them increasingly economically vulnerable in the face of recurring economic recessions. What are the long-term implications of this dispossession? Answering this question challenges laudatory tales of Mexico's economic growth after housing reform. Mexico's foreclosure crisis calls attention to the current push to create a nation of *individual* debtors and propagate Indigenous dispossession in the Global South through the rise of consumer debt, microfinance, and real estate markets.

1

Before Housing Reform
The Gendering of Urban Property

NEREIDA'S TOUR of her house in Cancún began with the land. Located in a new *región* (working-class neighborhood, also referred to as *colonia popular* or *colonia proletaria*), her *terreno* (land plot), measuring 160 square meters, was full of vegetation when she and her husband Emiliano were allotted the plot by the Housing Institute of the State of Quintana Roo (Instituto de la Vivienda del Estado de Quintana Roo or INVIQROO). This agency allocated affordable land plots to working-class families. "It was sad to cut back the *monte* (forest)," Nereida lamented, "but there was very little room to build a house." Her *matitas*—flowers and medicinal plants she cultivated from cuttings she brought back from Kuchmil—were beginning to provide groundcover for the dry, dusty soil. She hoped to soon have a garden as lush as her mother's garden in Kuchmil. In 2001, when this tour took place, most of the neighboring homes consisted of one-room *palapas* with roofs of corrugated tar paper, hastily constructed to cement land claims and thus prevent squatters (fig. 2). Relying on savings accrued over a decade spent working in Cancún, Nereida and Emiliano opted to build a one-bedroom concrete block house instead of a *palapa*, because this type of construction could withstand hurricanes and offered greater protection against theft. They planned to add a bathroom with indoor plumbing, extra bedrooms, and trees to provide shade from the unrelenting sun. For Nereida and Emiliano, land provided security because it made it possible to build a house that echoed life in Kuchmil and guaranteed them some autonomy from the economic downturns that plagued the tourist industry.

FIGURE 2. A self-built house in a new *región*. Photograph by author.

Emiliano acknowledged that his family would have remained landless if it were not for Nereida's activism. Eligibility for a land allotment through INVIQROO was restricted to families and single mothers. However, since land reserves are finite and the waitlists were long, it took years to get a government-subsidized land plot. To pressure the government to provide housing and install services like electricity, paved roads, water, and garbage removal in the *regiones*, families became actively involved with grassroots organizations mobilizing for land rights (Kray 2006). With the goal of obtaining a land plot, Nereida and Emiliano joined the grassroots organization Union of Independent Settlers (Unión de Colonos Independientes or UCI). Since organizations like UCI are structured around government patronage, they reward their most active members, who in this case were families who attended weekly meetings and invested a great deal of time supporting UCI's activities. For two years, Nereida attended weekly meetings, marched in political rallies, and registered new voters. Due to Nereida's political activism and commitment to UCI, her family was catapulted to the top of the list of members, granting them priority for a land plot. Nereida's activism became a template for Maya families to follow.

Nereida and Emiliano's story captures a snapshot of land policies prior to the implementation of neoliberal housing reforms. This chapter suggests that while the state (via INVIQROO) established a land redistribution program to address the housing needs of migrants, it based these programs on exclusionary ideologies of family, gender, and citizenship. By excluding Maya migrants who were unmarried and childless from affordable housing and land programs, the state defined citizenship narrowly and encouraged migrants to embrace the nuclear family if they wished to become citizens of this new urban space.[1] To lobby successfully for land, Maya women mobilized their status as wives and mothers. As they joined the movement for land rights in urban centers, Maya migrants from Kuchmil engaged with the state as "settlers," rather than as Indigenous people. Maya migrants' experiences with housing and land allotment programs illustrate not only the gender ideologies that buttress settler nation-state policies, but also the effects of these policies on gender relations and Indigenous activism.

Gendering Property

Quintana Roo has long been described as a "frontier zone," where Maya people were forcibly resettled into newly created towns during Spanish colonial rule, Spanish settlers established sugar plantations and a global trade in mahogany and chicle, the Mexican government carved out new *ejidos* for mestizo settlement, elite Mexican "pioneers" built an international tourist industry, and local unrest catapulted into one of the most successful Indigenous insurrections in Latin America.[2] The settler colonial logic of frontier making through Indigenous land expropriation becomes complicated when Indigenous peoples are positioned as settlers.[3] Chris Loperena (2017) suggests that the "politics of frontier making" is a racial project. In this chapter, I show how this project is also gendered.

As Carmen Deere and Magdalena León de Leal (2001) argue, access to property rights is a gendered process produced by the interplay among family, community, the economy, and the state. In Mexico, the gendering of land rights is made evident by women's roles in the ejido.[4] A collective landholding system established by the Revolutionary Constitution of 1917 and modeled on Indigenous systems of landholding, the ejido has regulated social, political, and economic relations among rural and Indigenous households. Article 200 of the 1971 Federal Law of Agrarian Reform explicitly gave women the right to ejido membership. Yet male heads of households make up the overwhelming majority of ejido membership. By the mid-1990s, women constituted only 15–30 percent of *ejidatarios* (Stephen 1997). Moreover, in 1992, revisions to Article 27 of the Mexican constitution made it legally possible for *ejidatarios*, typically male, to sell ejido land. This move toward privatization removed women and children from the decision-making process involved in land usage (Botey 1998). Access to land, then, represents a struggle for gender equity for rural Mexican and Indigenous women.

In contrast to the abundant research on rural Mexican women's rights to property, very little work has been done on the gendering of property in Mexico's cities, especially cities like Cancún, whose exponential growth is a direct result of Indigenous migration.[5] What role does gender play in access to property rights in urban settings? In her study of property rights in Guadalajara, Mexico, Ann Varley (2010) finds that family relationships, more so than individual rights, determine rights to property. Women are more likely to own property, Varley explains, based on their status as wives and mothers. Varley's work suggests the importance of examining the gender and kinship ideologies that undergird property regimes. If we consider the settler nation-state as a deeply gendered, heteropatriarchal structure, as Native feminists propose (see Arvin et al. 2013; Baldy 2018; Speed 2019), how do these policies in turn shape gender relations among Maya migrants? Michel-Rolph Trouillot (2001) points out that we can see state "effects" by identifying the sets of processes and practices of individuals, governments, and institutions in local contexts. To locate the Mexican settler nation-state and trace its effects in Cancún prior to neoliberal housing reforms, I examine the land distribution policies administered by INVIQROO and migrants' engagement with these policies. By linking Maya migration to the property rights and gender and racial systems underpinning state institutions and policies, such as those enacted through INVIQROO, we can see the settler nation-state at work.[6]

Settling in Cancún

Prior to 2000, Maya migrants obtained housing in one of five ways: (1) renting small one-room dwellings, (2) squatting, (3) building a house on a relative's property, (4) purchasing land or a house through a private exchange, or (5) lobbying for land through the state's land redistribution program. In 2000, 30 percent of the population residing in the county of Benito Juárez, where Cancún is located, rented or borrowed housing (INEGI 2001, 434), resulting in an average occupancy of four persons per structure (INEGI 2000, 49). Much of this housing was located in the newly constructed *regiones* and shantytowns that mushroomed along the city's periphery. For Maya migrants, sharing housing reduced expenses and allowed them to send remittances to Kuchmil.

Leonardo's experience illustrates the difficulties migrants encountered finding housing in Cancún. The day after he graduated from ninth grade at the age of fifteen, Leonardo moved to Cancún. In the early hours of the morning, he boarded a bus to the city in the company of his older brother Horacio, who was already working as a bartender in a hotel in the Zona Hotelera.[7] His new home consisted of a tiny one-room wooden structure with a corrugated tar paper roof located in the backyard of a house.[8] This room, which he shared with Horacio and another Maya migrant, was located in one of the *regiones* on the edge of the city's commercial district. To help pay rent, his cousin found Leonardo a job as a janitor in the hotel where he worked.

Rising housing costs were increasingly consuming a larger portion of migrants' monthly salaries. In 1998, the average rent for a room was US$40 per month,[9] but Leonardo, who by then was working as a steward (a waiter's assistant), earned only about US$59 (excluding tips) per month.[10] By 2001, rent had increased to an average of US$100 per month, and Leonardo was earning US$65 (excluding tips) as an assistant bartender in another hotel. Since the cost of one month's rent exceeded Leonardo's monthly salary, he shared housing with friends and family members. By 2001, Leonardo had moved at least six times.[11] At this time, he was sharing a small room with a Maya coworker. This room was part of a long, rectangular, concrete building that had been subdivided into four rooms with their individual bathrooms and entrances, one of two buildings that had been squeezed onto the land-lord's house plot. It was located a block away from his brother Horacio's home. After six years of migrating throughout Cancún's shantytowns in search of dignified and affordable living accommodations, Leonardo had begun saving to purchase a plot of land in Cancún.

For migrants in Cancún, owning a parcel of land is crucial for survival because it provides a stable place of residence throughout the fluctuat-ing tourist seasons. During the low season (between September and mid-December), hotels experience a decline in hotel occupancy. To minimize costs, hotels reduce staff by refusing to renew contracts with short-term employees. The lack of income makes it very difficult for the working class, who are typically employed in these positions as waiters, bartenders, and cooks, to pay their rent during the low tourist season. Among Maya migrants from Kuchmil, those who save enough money during the high season wait out the low season, but those who have not return to their natal villages. Owning one's home makes it easier to remain in Cancún continuously and to sponsor relatives seeking work in this city.

For Maya migrants from the ejido community of Kuchmil who now reside in Cancún, the impetus for land ownership was not derived from capitalism's emphasis on private ownership, but rather originated in their family's history of debt peonage prior to the Caste War and their own experiences with the ejido (Castellanos 2010a, 2010b). Their grandparents worked as *peones* on haciendas before the Maya uprising that became known as the Caste War of 1847. During the war, they fled from debt peonage and settled in southeastern Yucatán, an area abandoned by mestizos during the war. With the establishment of the ejido system, their rights to work the land in this area were formally recognized by the Mexican government. Because of these experiences, land for this Indigenous community has come to represent a primary source of food, freedom from slavery, and autonomy from the state. Not surprisingly, Kuchmil migrants attach many of these meanings onto land in Cancún, thus transforming the meaning of land from private property (as recognized by the state) into a symbol of freedom and autonomy from tourism, debt peonage, and the state.

Purchasing land or a home, however, is very difficult to manage on a hotel employee's salary. The value of finished homes and the land on which they were built, particularly if the land includes basic services such as electricity, a sewage system, and access to running water, has increased dramatically over the past three decades. To purchase developed property requires large amounts of cash and credit. For example, in 2001, a new two-bedroom house cost about US$30,000 if paid in full at the moment of purchase.[12] With the financing of a thirty-year mortgage, the price increased exponentially to an estimated US$300,000. Undeveloped land was significantly cheaper, especially if it was located in an undeveloped neighborhood; the lack of a housing structure and basic infrastructure (i.e., roads and schools) reduced its cost considerably. On the private market, *terrenos baldíos* (undeveloped land) retailed for US$3,000–US$6,000 and required a deposit of US$300–US$500 and a fee of US$200 to transfer the title. The remaining balance was typically paid in monthly installments over a three-to-eight-year period.[13] The plot sizes of *terrenos baldíos* varied; for example, a plot measuring 320 square meters was priced at US$5,000. Since few Maya migrants had the capital necessary for this kind of investment, they turned to INVIQROO.

Subsidizing Property

In 1972, the federal government established public agencies like INFONAVIT and the Social Security Institute's Housing Fund for Federal Government Employees (Fondo de la Vivienda del Instituto de Seguridad y Servicios Sociales de los Trabajadores del Estado or FOVISSSTE) to address the housing needs of its citizens. However, most Maya migrants did not earn enough or had not worked long enough to accumulate the credits necessary to qualify for a home loan offered through these programs.[14] After the early 1980s, the reduction in government subsidies to these public housing agencies, the increase in inflation and the cost of housing materials, and stagnant minimum wages further eroded the purchasing power of lower-income households (Gilbert and Varley 1991). To prevent the development of irregular housing such as squatter settlements, the government has actively engaged in directing land development in its cities. In states where the population has grown exponentially, alternative institutions and policies have been created to address the working poor's housing needs.

In 1984, the state of Quintana Roo established INVIQROO to curb the growth of irregular housing and provide access to housing for the populations residing in hastily constructed dwellings (*Diario Oficial*, March 9, 1984). This state agency was charged with overseeing urban development (both tourism and commercial) to benefit local commerce and working-class families.[15] INVIQROO's objective was to provide "dignified and decent homes" for the state's working-class residents by distributing land plots to residents with access to limited resources (*Diario Oficial*, March 9, 1984). It did so by administering the redistributions of the state's national land reserves. In Cancún, INVIQROO's efforts focused primarily on securing land to meet the housing needs of working-class residents. INVIQROO was also responsible for building the basic infrastructure, such as electricity, running water, schools, and parks, necessary to integrate these *colonias* (neighborhoods) into the city's urban zone, but this typically happened at least one year after land had been subdivided and sold. An INVIQROO land grant consisted of a ten-year mortgage at a 10 percent interest rate for 160 square meters lots, and required that a home be built on it within one year, which resulted in self-help housing in colonias without basic services (Ward 1982).

Nereida and Emiliano recalled that they spent one year without electricity and water. They relied on candles and purchased water from tanker trucks that periodically dispersed water in the *regiones*. In 2001, recipients provided a down payment of approximately US$380 and signed a contract with the state to pay US$4,783 for the land over a ten-year period. Repayment of this loan consisted of monthly payments of US$44. In January 2002, 6,200 applications were pending at INVIQROO, of which only 2,500 had been assigned a parcel of land.[16] The overwhelming demand for land forced INVIQROO to "operate like a resilience and perseverance test, where applicants waited three to four years for a parcel of land."[17] Despite the long waiting period, INVIQROO's representative Edgar Campos García informed me that the city of Cancún provided land at a faster rate than most other states.

Land availability impinged on the length of the waiting period. Initially, the state's land reserves were derived from national forests, but as the forests dwindled, the agency periodically expropriated ejido lands that surrounded the city, from which it carved out subsidized land plots for Cancún's working class. The 1992 revisions to Article 27 of the constitution, however, made it possible for ejido land to be sold instead of expropriated. Prior to the revisions, ejido land had been conceptualized as inalienable; members had usufruct rights only.[18] The new agrarian law, however, permitted ejidos to be divided up among its members as long as two-thirds of its members agreed to do so. *Ejidatarios* near Cancún took advantage of privatization to sell their lands at a profit to the state, private enterprises, and individuals. However, the cost of these lands was prohibitive for INVIQROO. The institute depended primarily on the state and federal governments for funding and relied on the government's right to expropriate land for the public good as a mechanism by which to acquire land.[19] *Ejidatarios* were compensated, but not at the market rate. In 2000, INVIQROO's land reserve included 3,846.49 hectares of land spread throughout the state, of which only 460.87 hectares were located in the municipality of Benito Juárez and the adjacent municipality of Isla Mujeres (*Revista Peninsular* 2000). The agency was short 1,700 hectares of projected demand (Kray 2006). In 2002, to increase its land reserves, INVIQROO began negotiating with the ejidos Isla Mujeres and Alfredo V. Bonfil to expropriate over 2,500 hectares of land.[20]

Acquiring land through INVIQROO required more than just patience and perseverance. Applicants had to meet a host of qualifications to participate in this program: (1) be married by civil registry or in a common-law marriage that could be verified with receipts demonstrating cohabitation, (2) be registered to vote in Cancún, (3) own no other property in Cancún, and (4) provide proof of residence in Cancún verified through an official letter from the *ayuntamiento* (municipal government office). INVIQROO's representatives extolled the progressive character of this agency because, unlike INFONAVIT, it did not limit land distribution to those with a history of work in the formal sector. However, although applicants were not officially required to provide proof of economic stability (at least this was not one of the qualifications the representatives mentioned), they were asked to submit an employment contract or a letter from an employer demonstrating proof of employment. Once applicants were informed that they had been assigned parcels of land, they were required to secure their contracts with down payments of US$380. Therefore, this review process limited applicants to a particular sector of workers from Cancún.

Controlling Migration

In Mexico as in many other Latin American countries, the ideology of homeownership has been used as a mechanism for social control of the middle class and the poor (Eckstein 1977; Gilbert and Varley 1991; Ward 1982). The state of Quintana Roo was no exception. Housing played a central role in shaping the contours of membership and belonging in Cancún. It positioned Maya migrants as settlers and deracialized them as political subjects. Maya Migrants were not allowed to engage the state as Indigenous subjects. Instead, they were transformed into citizens who made claims as political subjects to the state of Quintana Roo. Although access to housing made it possible for the state to establish a permanent workforce for its tourist economy, the ideology of homeownership was oriented toward specific sectors of Mexico's population and was conflated with the nuclear patriarchal family. A careful examination of the INVIQROO's prerequisites reveals the exclusionary ideologies underlying state land distribution policies and highlights the state's regard for nuclear families as the primary beneficiaries of subsidized housing.

For INVIQROO, belonging to a family was the "fundamental" attribute that shaped its applicant pool.[21] *Family* was defined as a married heterosexual nuclear household or, alternatively, as a household made up of a single mother and her offspring. As a result, migrants who did not conform to this vision were excluded from this program. INVIQROO claimed not to discriminate against common-law marriage, but the majority of its recipients were married couples with children. This outcome may also be due to the difficulties couples faced in verifying cohabitation if they were childless or did not have paperwork confirming their union. For example, for couples living in unofficial rental housing, written rental agreements were uncommon, and payment receipts to substantiate claims of cohabitation were difficult to obtain. For the state, the presence of children played a critical role in determining who received land, because in practice family was defined as a married couple with a child, preferably a child who was born in Cancún and thereby considered a citizen of the state of Quintana Roo. Since families with children were prioritized, married couples without children found themselves at the bottom of the waiting list. Nereida and Emiliano had two children, both born in Cancún, when they were allotted their land plot. Single men like Leonardo and most single women—except those with children who met all the other requirements—did not qualify.

A narrow window of income earnings also limited participation in INVIQROO. The migrant poor who had a difficult time finding employment and were relegated to the informal employment sector or to short-term contract work were disqualified (Cornelius 1975). The state perceived them as incapable of meeting the monthly payments and therefore too risky an investment. At the same time, migrants who worked in the informal sector who earned salaries equivalent to those as hotel employees were not eligible unless they could demonstrate proof of stable employment. Similarly, migrants employed in the formal sector were usually ineligible if they earned enough credits to qualify for housing through INFONAVIT.[22] Through this process of documentation, the state ensured that the families who received subsidized housing included a male provider capable of sustaining a nuclear household.

Due to its efforts to incorporate the working poor into the state's urban development, INVIQROO was considered a "progressive" agency.[23] Yet this progressive character was not as all-embracing as the agency's representatives claimed. INVIQROO did more than just hand out land to needy families. It relied on the images of the nuclear family and the good worker to determine who would be the future landowning citizens of Cancún. In addition to adhering to the moral framework of a family-centered ideology, applicants were also required to register to vote in Cancún and show proof of the ability to hold long-term employment contracts. Migrants had to demonstrate their transformation from peasants (conceptualized as backward and primitive) into stable diligent workers (conceptualized as modern). Through this agency, the state played a critical role in shaping the future of Cancún. By regulating the growth of the city's periphery, it determined which migrants could become property owners. It pressured

Maya migrants to establish permanent residency in Cancún and converted them into deracialized subjects, thereby introducing a formal relationship with the state that was no longer bound by revolutionary mandates.

Reifying Gender Relations

In rural Yucatán, the ejido serves as the basis for social organization. The *palapa,* more than just a form of shelter, serves as the ideological cornerstone of rural life (Redfield and Villa Rojas 1934). Families cultivate corn, squash, and beans for consumption. Traditionally work is typically split between men who work in the cornfields and women who care for children and tend gardens on their house plots. Young men and women were expected to marry and start a nuclear family by the age of twenty-five. However, as the ejido was reduced to sub-subsistence due to ecological degradation, climate change, and overpopulation, migration became a way to sustain ejido life. With the onset of migration, the gendered division of labor became increasingly difficult to sustain. Beginning in the 1970s, to supplement farmwork, men began to migrate seasonally to augment their income, while women remained at home. In the 1980s, male migrants began settling in Cancún. In 1991, after a severe drought, young women joined them. This exodus has normalized migration as an adolescent rite of passage. While life in Cancún is not regulated by the ejido, the ideological principles of reciprocity, communality, and a gendered division of labor remain salient for Maya migrants, who find creative ways to incorporate them into urban life.

For some Maya women, these principles have prompted them to redefine what it means to be a woman, wife, and mother in Cancún. As Maya women entered Cancún's labor force, they were able to earn and save money. Married women pooled their income with their husbands to support their families needs. Unmarried women sent remittances to their natal households. As these women became key contributors to their households, they were granted equal say in household decision-making processes both in Kuchmil and in Cancún. They were also given more freedom to travel and move around the city without a chaperone. These women encouraged their siblings to go to high school (in some cases even college) by paying their fees and tuition. Nereida, for example, sent money home to help pay her younger brother's high school and college tuition. Given these new obligations, migrant women postponed marriage to continue supporting their natal households, unlike migrant men, who married at a young age and soon after stopped sending remittances. For Maya women, living and working in Cancún came to be equated with physical and economic autonomy.

In spite of the surge in female autonomy, migration also led to a reification of gender relations that dovetailed with INVIQROO's expectations. Because Maya men usually married by their midtwenties, they bolstered the model of the nuclear family that held sway in their natal community and that was promoted by the state. Although they agreed with the need for greater equality between the sexes and encouraged their sisters to find work in Cancún, these young men opted to have their wives stay home to care for their children and thus maintained a gendered division of labor. This model of gender relations also made it easier to lobby for land. Navigating INVIQROO's bureaucracy took up a lot of time; applicants met frequently with bureaucrats to plead their cases and impress upon them their need for land. In exchange for migrants' political affiliation and activism, grassroots settler organizations like UCI served as an intermediary with INVIQROO and other public officials. Government agencies like INVIQROO relied on organizations like UCI to help petitioners fill out their applications and organize paperwork. Christine Kray calls this process the "bureaucratization of political patronage" because organizations like UCI and Only Settlers' Front (Frente Único de Colonos or FUC) also co-opt political protests on behalf of politicians (2006, 68). Since Maya men worked six days a week, sometimes double shifts, this type of political engagement on their part was impossible. This task fell to their wives, who gathered and submitted the paperwork to INVIQROO and became active members in grassroots organizations. By exiting the workforce, these women were able to advocate for land on behalf of their families.[24]

Jovana's story is illustrative of this process. In 2000, while working in Cancún as a domestic servant, Jovana married a migrant from Kuchmil. Soon after, she became pregnant and quit her job. She and her husband, Juan, shared a one-room apartment rental with her sister. After the birth of their son in 2001, they submitted an application to INVIQROO. Nereida's success inspired them to join UCI. To pressure the government to provide land to its most active members, UCI trained its members in tactics that would get them access to politicians. When Jovana and Juan first joined UCI, they were ranked at the bottom of a membership roll of approximately one hundred fifty families. Since Juan worked full-time, Jovana was responsible for attending UCI meetings and events. By participating in UCI-sponsored activities, Jovana earned points that improved her standing on this list. She walked precincts to register voters and contributed twenty pesos each week to cover membership dues. At political rallies, she joined hundreds of migrants who chanted "We see! We Feel! UCI is here!" (*¡Se ve, se siente, el UCI está presente!*). With a young infant in tow, Jovana found canvassing door to door to be exhausting work. This level of dedication and participation was a challenge for Jovana to sustain, but she persevered because her husband joined her when possible. Through her active membership in UCI, Jovana drastically shortened INVIQROO's waiting period. In June 2002, one year after submitting her application, Jovana and Juan were rewarded for her activism with a land grant from INVIQROO.

As Maya women became key players in the settlement process, they established strong relationships with political leaders and bureaucrats. They learned to maneuver bureaucracies like the government's National System for Integral Family Development (Sistema Nacional para el Desarrollo Integral de la Familia or DIF) which was dedicated to improving women's and children's welfare. These engagements with a wider social network alleviated the extreme loneliness Maya women experience; with only their children for company, married women usually spend most of the day (or nights if their husbands worked in discotheques) confined to their one-room apartments. Nereida acknowledged that she learned to be less reserved and "afraid" after knocking on strangers' doors during voter registration drives. She learned to assert herself and speak up for herself. Although these activities gave women the opportunity to learn about their rights as citizens in Cancún, this engagement was constructed on the basis of their status as mothers and wives, not as Indigenous people. Nereida quit working with UCI soon after receiving her land plot; she noted that the organization itself was dismantled a few years later. Nonetheless, participation in these organizations and institutions reinforced the prominence of the nuclear heteronormative family and motherhood as the context within which Kuchmil migrants engaged with the state.

On the Margins of the State

In contrast, unmarried, childless Maya women and men who wished to settle permanently in Cancún were marginalized by the nation-state's efforts to transform migrants into citizens and settlers through land ownership. Leonardo's experience with INVIQROO illustrates this process. By 2001, Leonardo was tired of renting apartments. Renting, he explained, "isn't the same [as owning a home]" because landlords "prohibit us from making any scandal. They prohibit heavy drinking, loud noise, or bringing friends to drink in your house." The privacy Leonardo sought had to be purchased, but as a single, childless male with a short employment history (six years) in Cancún he did not qualify for a land grant through INVIQROO or a house through INFONAVIT, and he was not ready to get married. He wanted to buy a parcel of land and build his home first to provide himself with a bit of autonomy from the fluctuations of the market. In Kuchmil, young men usually built their homes next to their father's house or on a plot provided by the ejido. In Cancún, Leonardo's brothers built their homes on their in-laws' properties. Leonardo's options were limited to either purchasing a property or getting married to become eligible for land from INVIQROO.

For migrants who remained unmarried, their status prevented them from receiving state support to acquire land. Similar to ejido communities, single women residing in cities had few opportunities to become property owners. I did not encounter any grassroots organization that provided support for these migrants' efforts to acquire land. At this time, most unmarried Maya migrants preferred to maintain their political affiliations and voter registration cards in their natal states, where they could mobilize established ties with state and municipal agencies to garner resources, instead of transferring this allegiance to Cancún and the state of Quintana Roo, where resources were scarce and political patronage often results in stalled or co-opted social movements.

The process of transforming Indigenous migrants into "settlers" involves contradictory messages between how the state defines the contours of its imagined community and migrants' everyday practices. Government-funded organizations like INVIQROO provide the cheapest alternative for land acquisition, but local politics, heavy bureaucracy, long waiting periods, and economic and social criteria reduce the probability of land acquisition for many migrants. Although housing reform made it easier for unmarried men and women to purchase homes, exclusionary family and gender ideologies continue to undergird these programs. These ideologies shape how state land redistribution programs function and who gets access to housing. Participating in state-sponsored land allotment programs required Maya migrants to document their transformation into modern citizens. In the process, gender relations among migrants were reified by state policies and organizations rooted in images of the family as a heteronormative and patriarchal nuclear structure. These policies mark other relationships, such as same-sex unions, as undesirable. Moreover, they conflate the heteronormative family with citizenship and national belonging and thereby exclude migrants who do not conform with this ideal. Understanding settlement among Maya migrants, then, requires an interrogation of the ideological notions that underpin settler state policies and the way in which these policies shape migrants' settlement practices.

Transitions

In 2002, due to the change in administrations after local elections, the state changed the name INVIQROO to Institute for the Development of Housing and Property Regularization (Instituto de Fomento a la Vivienda y Regularización de la Propiedad or INFOVIR). Its functions expanded to include land regularization of ejido land plots sold through private transactions. In 2004, Quintana Roo established the Institute of State Patrimony (Instituto del Patrimonio Estatal or IPAE) to centralize the distribution of the state's land reserves (national, state, and municipal). INFOVIR oversaw urban development, but it was divested of its right to administer the state's national land reserves and was dependent on IPAE for access to these reserves.[25] On September 30, 2013, INFOVIR ceased to exist; the Ministry of Urban Development and Housing (Secretaría de Desarollo Urbano y Vivienda or SEDUVI) became responsible for land regularization and urban development in Cancún.[26] But regulating informal colonias or squats remained under the purview of the Committee for the Regulation of Land Tenure (Comisión para la Regularización de la Tenencia de la Tierra or CORETT). As land reserves become finite, the possibility of land ownership has been foreclosed for much of Cancún's working poor. A SEDUVI representative explained that the "lack of land was one of the greatest problems facing Cancún." To resolve this problem, the government turned to social housing, a plan that came with its own set of troubles.

2

Promoting Housing Reform
Debt as Patrimony

CONSTRUCTED IN 2005, the *fraccionamiento* Paseos Kabah is one of many social housing developments built to provide "dignified" housing for low-income residents of Cancún (fig. 3). *Fraccionamientos* (subdivisions) are planned communities, repetitive in their sameness and radiating out from the city's periphery. To make them affordable, they are built cheaply and quickly, using the smallest footprint per unit possible.[1] Hailed as the cornerstone of Mexico's future economic prosperity, these developments embodied the physical manifestation of the neoliberal shift to decenter land and replace it with the house. While housing construction did stimulate Mexico's economy (although who benefited remains controversial), it also generated in its wake a series of crises—environmental and economic, local and national. To narrate the crises it begat, I juxtapose two events that took place in Paseos Kabah. The first involves former President Vicente Fox and his housing plan, and the second centers on one Maya migrant's desire for national belonging in neoliberal Mexico. Both events took place soon after Hurricane Wilma.

Within a year of its opening, Paseos Kabah faced the onslaught of a Category 4 storm with a windspeed of 150 mph (240 km/h). Hurricane Wilma devastated Cancún's infrastructure, damaging over two-thirds of hotels and several thousand homes. The city went one week without electricity and running water. As one of Mexico's most popular tourist sites, generating over US$2 billion in revenues in 2005, rebuilding Cancún became a national priority. President Vicente Fox considered access to housing one of the key ways of helping Cancún "get back on its feet" after the devastation

FIGURE 3. Paseos Kabah housing development. Photograph by author.

of this calamity. On a warm day in February 2006, with this mission in mind, Fox gave a speech before a large crowd in Paseos Kabah. He spoke about Wilma's devastation, but the main purpose of this visit was to preside over a ceremony in which four hundred families would receive the titles to their new homes and to honor FOVISSSTE, the government agency that provided them with their mortgages. FOVISSSTE participates in the federal government's providence fund, which requires employers to contribute 5 percent over and above the value of an employee's wages to this fund. This credit can be used toward a down payment on a home.[2] President Fox critiqued the irresponsibility of previous administrations that contributed to Mexico's fiscal crises. In contrast, he affirmed his commitment to give every Mexican "the opportunity to secure a *patrimonio* (patrimony)."[3] To achieve this mandate, Fox agreed to build 750,000 houses and fund 750,000 home loans during the last ten months of his administration.[4]

Horacio, whom I introduced in the previous chapter, benefited from Fox's mandate by being one of the first people to purchase a one-bedroom tract home in Paseos Kabah. Horacio arrived in Cancún as a teenager to work in the tourism industry. Since he spent nearly two decades saving money to buy a house, Horacio was "filled with excitement" to purchase a "modern" home with a loan from INFONAVIT and the private mortgage lender Hipotecaria Su Casita. But the 2008 global economic recession severely impacted tourism, making it difficult for Horacio to make his mortgage payments. By 2011, he was facing foreclosure. These two events—a celebratory ceremony of homeownership in the wake of a hurricane and a potential loss of a home plagued by acrimonious foreclosure proceedings—speak to a critical dissonance between a nation and its citizens, global capital and consumers, and most importantly, between Indigenous peoples and the state. Indeed, threats of foreclosure led Horacio to question and critique national efforts to associate patrimony with debt.

This chapter examines the transformation of Mexico's land distribution policies and property rights through a discursive analysis of the ideologies central to government campaigns promoting "dignified" housing. According to the Federal Housing Law, "dignified" housing adheres to national safety standards, is resistant to natural disasters, and provides access to basic services. Acknowledging that housing is a contested site for the politics of gendered propriety, suburban domesticity, and citizenship (Lobo 1982; Murphy 2015; Lopez 2015), I evaluate the narrative devices and rhetorical strategies used to make housing attractive and to align debt with national ideals. The Fox administration considered access to housing key to helping Cancún recover after Hurricane Wilma in 2005. During the inauguration of one of Cancún's first housing projects, Fox committed to giving Mexicans a patrimony in the form of a "dignified" home. In this context, patrimony refers to private home. By evoking the concept of patrimony, Fox deliberately conflates the private housing market with institutions like the *ejido*. This chapter examines this conflation and the ideological shift in values it marks by drawing parallels between the campaign's "social life" and a Maya family's decision to purchase a home. I suggest that the language of patrimony and suburban domesticity, intended to soften the retreat of the state from land redistribution, makes the process of going into debt on a much larger scale than previously possible both palatable and desirable.

The Shifting Meanings of Patrimony

Fox uses the language of patrimony to talk about a private home. Yet what was being handed out that day—home loans and physical structures—could not be called patrimony in the traditional sense in Mexico. According to anthropologist Elizabeth Ferry, patrimony in Mexico is typically conceived as a "collective, exclusive possession by a social group, often organized or conceptualized as a kin group" and handed down through generations (2002, 331). As a shared bundle of rights to resources, patrimony "works as an idiom and set of practices that constrain exchange by classifying patrimonial possessions as ideally inalienable: Such possessions are meant to remain within the control of the social group that lays claim to them" (Ferry 2002, 331). A classic example of patrimony is the ejido, land held collectively and which prior to the 1992 ejido reform was inalienable. The ejido system was a postrevolutionary phenomenon initially modeled after collective landholding communities (also called ejidos) during the colonial period, making up the *república de indios*. After the 1910 Mexican Revolution, postrevolutionary administrations relied heavily on the revolutionary mandates of land and liberty to incorporate Indigenous peasants and laborers into their political base and legitimate their regimes. Land redistribution in the form of ejidos became central to this process. In Yucatán, from 1915 to 1933, the state government reallocated one-fifth of farmland to its peasantry. In 1931, Horacio's hometown of Kuchmil, in conjunction with three of its neighbors (Chan Sahkay, Ke'eldzonot, and Katzim), was allocated an ejido grant.

In spite of the 1992 constitutional reform that permitted the privatization of ejido land (and thus paved the way for NAFTA), 57 percent of land in Yucatán continues to be owned collectively.[5] Communities like Kuchmil that depend on slash-and-burn agriculture reject privatization because the ejido continues to be the most efficient steward of its natural resources and its collective well-being. As don Patricio, a community elder, explained, "The rich are the ones to benefit [from privatization]. . . . By not dividing the ejido, we can leave it to our children. It's their patrimony." According to Ferry, patrimony becomes more than a way to organize labor and production. It becomes a moral framework through which claims over resources can be made. It must be noted that efforts to privatize the ejido are ongoing, especially as urban areas expand—Mexico will be 75 percent urban by the year 2030—and as rural land prices rise in value.

While home loans gave working-class individuals and families access to a physical structure (a house), this deed did not transform these homes into inalienable possessions or a collective resource. Rather, these twenty-five-year home loans (home prices in social housing developments ranged between US$23,000 and US$25,000 in 2005) placed working-class individuals and families deeply in debt to several creditors: the private development companies like Grupo Sadasi, the federal government that underwrites INFONAVIT and FOVISSSTE loans, and the private nonbank housing finance companies like Hipotecaria Su Casita that supplement federal loans. Until these homes are paid off, homeowners are susceptible to threats of dispossession. How did Mexico move from the classic understanding of patrimony to a neoliberal one? Tracing the impetus for housing reform in Mexico illuminates this transformation.

Redeeming Culture, Reclaiming Land

The focus on patrimony and dignity is grounded in settler logics of dispossession aimed at dismantling cultural institutions that are considered to impede progress. For Fox, Mexico's land tenure system, a system that has been the hallmark of Indigenous policies since the Mexican Revolution, represented a paternalistic culture that was anachronistic to modernity. Fox explains,

> And we have this culture in rural areas of the ejidos [*sic*] system, [these] agrarian reforms that never gave away the land to be owned by the *campesinos* or the *ejidatarios*, and this is where [Peruvian economist] Hernando de Soto's philosophy comes into place. These *ejidatarios*, as long as they don't own that piece of land, they don't have a title on that piece of land, they will never be able to use it, to capitalize and to develop their business. This is why we are using Hernando de Soto's philosophy, starting with the ejidos system. *Ejidatarios* own their land, have a title, and can move ahead.[6]

Inspired by economist Hernando de Soto, Fox apprehends communal land-holdings as archaic systems that limit self-actualization. De Soto (2000) is well-known for championing private property as the solution for poverty in the so-called "Third World." Informal and communal land tenure systems, according to de Soto, are outmoded social contracts that prevent individuals from investing their capital to create surplus value. Formalization, the legalization of private property rights, restores order to the disorder of the "Third World" and transforms the poor into productive *individuals*. "By transforming people with property interests into accountable individuals, formal property created individuals from masses," de Soto explains. "People no longer needed to rely on neighborhood relationships or make local arrangements to protect their rights to assets. Freed from primitive economic activities and burdensome parochial constraints, they could explore how to generate surplus value from their own assets" (2000, 54). Doing away with cultural practices that hinder individual responsibility and accountability, according to de Soto, is imperative in order for capitalism to thrive. The ejido is an example of this type of system, especially as ejidos have become increasingly unsustainable and find it difficult to compete with global markets. Neoliberal policies intent on overhauling and modernizing the ejido system are based on de Soto's endorsement of private property. Privatizing ejido lands, the government argued, would remove the impediments that restrict how *ejidatarios* imagine market relations. It is individual, not collective, property rights that will kindle seismic shifts in how the poor relate to capital. In this push toward market fundamentalism, Fox ignores that his reference to "culture" is not just a question of habitus, of altering a worldview constrained by "primitive" practices. In the case of the state of Yucatán, where the majority of ejidos remain communal and are administered by Indigenous *pueblos*, the culture of collective land ownership is rooted in Indigenous practices shaped by a history of land dispossession and ecological disasters (Castellanos 2010b). *Ejidatarios* in Yucatán are not stuck in the past but instead rely on the past to inform their relationships to the land, each other, and capital.

Framing a culture of communal land use as deficient, as Fox does, forms part of a settler and colonial logic of improvement that considered "vacant," uncultivated, "underused," unmarked, and common land as land that could be justifiably expropriated (Farris 1984; Chang 2010, 2011; Cronon 1983). To justify his argument, de Soto (2000) calls forth images of pioneers and the settler colonial logic of improvement when he equates present-day so-called Third World economies with the nineteenth-century United States, when pioneers sought to make formal claims on Indigenous lands in the Wild West. Similarly, ejidos are deemed a prime "frontier market," a ready-made laboratory for enacting de Soto's ethos of privatization. Approximately 55.6 percent of national lands are held communally in Mexico, marking 27,541 ejidos and close to 103 million hectares as potential sites for privatization and thus vulnerable to predation (https://www.land-links.org/country-profile/mexico/#land).

Quintana Roo is a case in point for this extractivist logic. As the last territory to be granted statehood in 1974, it has one of the lowest population densities and highest forest cover (67 percent) in the nation under communal ownership and management (Ellis et al. 2014). Prior to NAFTA, development of these lands was regulated by government institutions like INVIQROO, INFOVIR, and the National Fund for the Development of Tourism (Fondo Nacional de Fomento al Turismo or FONATUR) (Rueda

Estrada and Fiorentini Cañedo 2015). Privatization, however, has converted Quintana Roo's vast ejido lands into potential sites for development, in this case social housing.

Promoting a "Property-Owning Democracy"

Fox's promotion of social housing has caught on among private financial institutions, development agencies like the World Bank, and the very people this housing is intended to serve. Of Mexico's 26.7 million households, only 17.8 million own what the government considers to be an "adequate" house. Over 50 percent of Mexican homes are self-built. Not surprisingly, the private real estate market in Mexico is booming. In 2005, real estate sales earned more than US$16 billion.[7] In 2017, housing constituted 5.9 percent of the country's GDP and generated an annual investment of US$25.1 billion, while INFONAVIT managed a US$7 billion fund.[8] In the state of Quintana Roo where Cancún is located, the real estate industry is the most important sector after tourism and generates 15 percent of the state's GDP. As one of Mexico's fastest growing cities, Cancún is one of the main sites for this financial expansion. Financiers explain this growth as a response to the opening up of the market that began with the onset of NAFTA in 1994, but I suggest that this boom also needs to be contextualized within the changing meanings of debt, risk, and citizenship in modern Mexico. This shift is connected to Mexico's history of economic crises followed by periods of deregulation as economic reform.

For economist Drucilla Barker, the financialization of the economy is a story of not just wealth creation but also debt and debt creation, beginning with the "Third World" debt crisis that has deep implications for women and minorities.[9] She points out that mainstream discussions of the crisis fail to consider that debt creation necessitates creating "a new pool of debtors," a process that first began in the Global South in the 1970s with sovereign nations and that shifted to women, minorities, and the working poor in the United States in the 1980s. Barker reminds us that the austerity measures that countries in the Global South were forced to adopt disproportionately affected women and children and didn't save money. The dismantling of the welfare state and the elimination of subsidies displaced these costs onto the backs of the working poor, who absorbed cuts in childcare, food subsidies, employment, and benefits.

Indeed, the 1994 peso crisis and bank crisis devastated Mexico's economy. During the first six months, more than one million workers became unemployed (Otero 1996). Over 56,000 families lost their savings.[10] Inflation caused interest rates on home loans to skyrocket. Pressured by the International Monetary Fund (IMF), the government sped up the implementation of and deepened the neoliberal economic policies initially adopted to resolve the 1982 oil and debt crisis. These reforms included privatizing state-owned enterprises, promoting free trade by reducing tariffs, increasing export production, capping wages, reducing spending on social programs like low-income housing, and instituting bank interest rates of 60 percent (Otero 1996). As banks put in place strict requirements about who could qualify for credit, the number of mortgages and amount of credit available was drastically reduced, excluding much of Mexico's working class and a large sector of its middle class. As inflation rose and people lost faith in banks, they relied increasingly on each other as way to generate and produce credit in the forms of small loans or *tandas* (rotating credit associations) (see Hellman 1995). Mexico "has one of the lowest credit ratio[s] to GDP, in comparison to other countries in Latin America" (Levy Orlik and Domínguez Blancas 2011, 15).

In response to this gap in the housing market, nonbank finance companies stepped in to provide home loans.[11] These niche intermediary lenders, known as Financial Societies of Limited Scope (Sociedades Financieras de Objeto Limitado or SOFOLes) were created in December 1993 by the Mexican government (with financing committed until 2009) to provide mortgage loans to low- and middle-income families and provide financing for developers building public housing projects (IFC 2007). Heavily subsidized by the Mexican government, the Inter-American Development Bank, and the World Bank's International Finance Corporation, SOFOLes became the mechanism by which to monetize surplus populations and made it possible for the state to withdraw from housing construction (Soederberg 2014). SOFOLes quickly came to disburse 21 percent of social housing loans (Bredenoord and Cabrera Montiel 2014).

By the time Fox became president in 2000, the IMF's austerity measures had stabilized Mexico's economy, but they, along with the 1992 ejido reform that ended state-administered land redistribution, made it impossible for millions of poor and working-class Mexicans to own or gain access to land. An estimated 40 percent of Mexican households do not qualify or have access to formal housing loans (Elias and Ritchie 2008). These landless masses presented a problem for Mexico's transformation into a modern nation. Fox's vision for Mexico entailed solving its housing deficit by transforming and restructuring Mexico's real estate market to attract foreign investment and thus generate new forms of wealth. To create a "property-owning democracy" ("Housing in Mexico" 2004), Fox instituted reforms to increase the working poor's access to housing.[12] These reforms included privatizing the real estate market and expanding the number of loans made available through public agencies like FOVISSSTE and INFONAVIT. INFONAVIT has become the largest mortgage supplier in Latin America. Like FOVISSSTE, this fund mandates contributions of 5 percent of worker's wages, which allows Mexicans to save toward a down payment on their future home. It also provides them with low-interest mortgages.[13] Fox considered housing for working-class citizens to be one of his administration's legacies. The belief that poverty and the lack of ownership precludes dignity, coupled with the demise of land redistribution, fueled the expansion of social housing. By advocating for housing over land, the Fox administration decentered land as the centerpiece of national belonging. Instead, home-ownership gained primacy in social programs aimed at helping the poor. In the process, Susanne Soederberg points out, "the fundamental causes of poverty, as well as the material bases of inequality, disappear behind the mask of freedom, equality, and democracy" (2014, 163).

In 2005, with the support of the Fox administration, INFONAVIT "agreed to authorize and jointly finance loans to workers with outside income, either as a result of tips or because their spouse is working."[14] Housing developers began building new homes that were affordable to the working class. Nonbank mortgage lenders like Hipotecaria Su Casita worked in tandem with developers like Grupo Sadasi to finance these homes. SOFOLes and developers were both heavily subsidized by the state (Soederberg 2014). SOFOLes like Su Casita acquired the bulk of this new market because they lent at an interest rate of 10 percent. And unlike private banks, they required smaller down payments, lent money to those employed in the informal economy, provided dollar-based loans to developers, and offered extended mortgages (twenty-five years versus the twenty-year mortgages provided by private banks) (IFC 2007).

Given the expanding potential of this market, private banks and finance companies soon invested in SOFOLes. In December 2005, Hipotecaria Su Casita, Mexico's largest SOFOL which was established in 1994 and was one of the funders for the housing project Paseos Kabah, had a net worth of US$182 million, with assets totaling to US$2.4 billion. In 2006, the Spanish bank Caja Madrid acquired a 40 percent stake in Su Casita.

The International Finance Corporation (IFC), a private sector arm of the World Bank Group, invested over US$300 million in SOFOLes, of which US$50 million went to Su Casita (IFC 2007).

By the early 1990s, as Julia Elyachar (2002) argues, the informal economy with its emphasis on individual entrepreneurship came to be seen by development agencies not only as cultural practices to emulate, but also as economic practices compatible with global finance and modern citizenship. In the case of Mexico's real estate market, with its deficit of over four million housing units in 2006 (IFC 2007), poverty reduction has become more than a way to improve people's lives. It has become a lucrative venture. Much of the country's urban growth has been propelled by self-help housing (Bredenoord and Cabrera Montiel 2014; Ward 1990, 1998), with 40 percent of Mexicans lacking what the government calls "dignified" or "adequate" housing (Elias and Ritchie 2008). In 2005, construction had become Mexico's most profitable sector, and in 2007, 86 percent of GDP was derived from housing stock replacement (Soederberg 2014). As Salvador Peniche, a researcher at the University of Guadalajara's Center for Business Management (Centro Universitario de Ciencias Económico Administrativas or CUCEA), succinctly stated, "Money is money, no matter where it comes from" (Herbert et al. 2012).

The new citizens of this "property-owning democracy" in Mexico are being molded in the image of individual property owners who are fiscally responsible and disciplined. IFC's mission to reduce poverty and "promote open and competitive markets in developing countries" is grounded in the idea of "help[ing] people help themselves."[15] The Mexican government and lending companies like SOFOLes have adopted this discourse of "individual responsibility" and "fiscal discipline" to explain national crises and economic progress. In Paseos Kabah, as Fox applauded the robust mortgage market, he cautioned the audience that the low interest rates were made possible by his government's "fiscal discipline." He criticized previous administrations for being "irresponsible and undisciplined" and for "not caring" about where and how they spent money or how much they borrowed, which as result caused 56,000 families to lose "all their patrimony" in 1995. According to Fox, "there is no way to progress without working, without all of you working, without the work of your families. . . . If we are all diligent, if we are all prudent, and we all take care . . . our families will no longer live in poverty and poverty won't touch that [second] generation."[16] This emphasis on responsibility and accountability harkens back to de Soto's emphasis on the need to "create individuals from masses" as the best way to extract capital

(2000, 54). Debt becomes what Miranda Joseph (2014) terms a "mode of accounting" that transforms social relations under neoliberalism.

In *Anti-Crisis*, Janet Roitman questions the telos of crisis that "evoke[s] a moral demand for a difference between the past and the future. And . . . the possibility for new forms of historical subjectivity" (2014, 8). For Roitman, "crisis" is a narrative device that "establishes the conditions of possible histories" and insists upon historical truths (2014, 11). Fox relied on the narrative of the 1994 crisis to make particular claims about Mexico's past, even as he urged its citizens to adopt a new vision for Mexico's future and in the process set up the conditions for a new history for land tenure in Mexico. Therefore, the only way for Mexico to progress was through fiscal discipline and hard work. Before this crowd of local government officials and working-class families, Fox directly linked fiscal discipline with individual responsibility and economic progress with private property. As a result, modernity becomes hinged to citizens' fiscal responsibility. Debt is considered to be good as long as no one defaults on their loan. But Fox disregards the fact that the Mexican state's retreat from land redistribution makes this type of modernity only possible to those willing to take on debt at the private individual level. Fox's use of the concept of patrimony serves as a key site for rethinking crisis and highlighting crisis's alignment with a long history of land dispossession and settler colonialism. As Jean O'Brien (2010) shows, narrative strategies like settler claims as the "first" and the "last" peoples to inhabit a place have served as powerful tools in effacing Indians from public memory and historical records in the United States. Using a similar sleight of hand, Fox relies on the concept of patrimony as a narrative device to associate debt with a revolutionary history and tradition of collective land ownership.

The 2008 global fiscal crisis resulted in a reduction in credit lines available from private banks to SOFOLes. Government subsidies from the Federal Mortgage Society (Sociedad Hipotecaria Financiera or SHF) expired in 2009. However given the growing demand for housing in Mexico, the Mexican government provided SOFOLes with a subsidy of Mex$16 billion to help stimulate housing construction in 2010. To attract investors, SOFOLes were taken over by other SOFOLes and large banks, and then they joined forces with corporations like Mabe, Mexico's leading appliance manufacturer. They also began to cater to emigrants with the aid of a government-funded program. In addition to its 171 offices in Mexico, Su Casita opened offices in Denver, Dallas, and Chicago.[17] By 2010, Su Casita had provided over 120,000 Mexicans living in Mexico and abroad with home loans.[18] That year Hipotecaria Su Casita announced it was mired in financial troubles. In 2011, Hipotecaria Patrimonios purchased Su Casita's loans. In January 2013, Su Casita formally declared bankruptcy.

A Nation of Individual Debtors

Proponents for a "property-owning democracy" have been deeply influenced by Peruvian economist Hernando de Soto's (1989) claims that democracy and capitalism cannot thrive without giving the poor access to de jure property rights. This emphasis on property rights aims to link the revolutionary ideals and Indigenous practices of land as patrimony with the free market and debt. As such, this emphasis on possession as investment occludes a pernicious history of dispossession that began with colonialism. Patrick Wolfe points out that in the United States, the Dawes Act "provided for a cultural transformation whereby the magic of private property ownership would propel Indians from the collective inertia of tribal membership into the progressive individualism of the American dream" (2006, 400). We continue to see remnants of this legacy of dispossession through the institutionalization of property regimes. In Mexico, the government's effort to create a robust real estate market is intended to buttress and institutionalize a property regime based on neoliberal market policies that erode or do away with Indigenous understandings of rights to communal property. Current efforts by the Mexican state can be read as a new iteration of a legacy of Indigenous dispossession.

Although neoliberal reforms have led to state retrenchment, the state continues to deeply influence everyday practices and collective action (Auyero 2012; Bourdieu 2005; Gupta 1995, 2012; Joseph and Nugent 1994; Miller and Rose 2013; Scott 1998, 2010). Drucilla Barker points out that the 2008 economic crisis led to what she calls a "deepening of indebtedness" that is "perpetuat[ing] lines of inequality along the lines of race, class, and gender." Barker urges scholars to address these issues by looking at the "systematic relationships among gender, race, and debt."[19] Thus, Barker draws our attention to the structures that created *nations in debt* in the Global South.

This inquiry of housing reform in Mexico questions recent laudatory tales of Mexico's economic success. It calls attention to the current push to create a *nation of individual debtors* in the Global South through the rise of consumer debt, microfinance, and real estate markets. As David Stoll (2013) has shown for Maya communities in Guatemala and Jan and Diane Rus (2014) have shown for Maya communities in Chiapas, easy access to microfinance has led to a vicious cycle of debt and dispossession that is intimately connected with migration to the United States and Indigenous desires for the American Dream. These studies point to the need for more ethnographies of privatized individualized indebtedness and the future implications of this type of debt servitude for struggling economies.

An Economic Albatross

I return to Horacio's story to illuminate how Maya migrants responded to the socializing mission of private lenders and development agencies. Maya migrants continually remind me that unlike village life, *todo es comprado* (everything must be purchased) in Cancún. To survive and acquire the trappings of modern life, Maya migrants have become indebted, even if this means falling prey to dispossession. Yet, as historian Jonathan Levy explains, risk is a morality tale that associates individual freedom with a dependence on corporate finance and the production of uncertainty and insecurity (2012, 6). For Maya migrants, the risk involved in taking on debt is a loss of autonomy through debt servitude and the loss of property through dispossession. Risk forms part of a moral framework where freedom has become inextricably tied to the financialization of life in Cancún. Yet given the declining productivity of farmwork, Maya communities have few options but to seek wage work in cities like Cancún. The experience of working and living in Cancún requires that Indigenous migrants negotiate their integration into this modernist project and its accompanying systems of global finance and credit.

Among the working class in Cancún, access to credit has been a recent phenomenon, but it forms part of finance's growing emphasis on predatory lending to the poor (Roy 2010; B. Williams 2004). Debt has become an integral part of being modern in Cancún, especially among working-class migrants. A few years ago, migrants like Horacio desired to own a home, but on their own terms, without debt. The story of how Horacio almost lost his home speaks to the shift in Maya migrants' relationship to property, transnational capital, and neoliberal reforms. What does Horacio's shift from rejecting debt to embracing it tell us about Indigenous cultural practices? When Horacio left Kuchmil at sixteen years of age, his older brother Reynaldo found him a job as a steward (waiter's assistant) in a hotel in Cancún. To save money, Horacio, Reynaldo, and a cousin rented a small room. Horacio sent money to his parents every couple of months. Until Horacio married in 1998, he alternated sharing housing with his brothers (Reynaldo, Enrique, and Leonardo) and a cousin. But after getting married, he and his wife Mari moved into one of the small rooms his father-in-law rented out. Instead of paying the standard monthly rental rate of US$40, they paid US$20. Horacio's father-in-law proposed that Horacio build a house in the back end of his property. He donated the land and Horacio paid for the building materials and construction. Horacio spent US$600 to build a house of only four square meters with a stone floor, wood planks for walls, and a roof of corrugated tar paper. He paid half of the utility bills but did not pay rent.

For Horacio, the desire for land stemmed from Kuchmil's longstanding history of mitigating dispossession. It was this desire that motivated Horacio to buy a plot of ejido land rather than purchase a home through INFON-AVIT. After nearly three years of living on his father-in-law's land, Horacio heard from a friend that one of the neighboring ejidos had privatized its land and was selling land parcels. Since Horacio's family had expanded with the births of two girls, they needed larger living quarters. "I can buy my things, but I don't have anywhere to put them," he explained. More importantly, he did not want his girls to grow up surrounded by neighbors in the adjacent rental units who drank heavily throughout the night. Horacio visited his friend's home in this newly founded neighborhood located two kilometers outside of Cancún's western perimeter. The owner of the property, a former *ejidatario*, assured Horacio that the colonia would soon be accessible by public transportation, and he promised that as soon as all the lots had been sold, he would build, with the aid of the city government, the infrastructure to connect the former ejido to public services like potable water and electricity. At the time, these plots were surrounded by lowland tropical jungle and lacked access to running water and electricity. The nearest bus stop was half a mile away on the main road. Initially, Horacio was concerned that the sale could be fraudulent, a case of an owner selling his land to several clients, but the ongoing construction by new owners and conversations with them convinced him this sale was legitimate. In 2001, Horacio and Mari placed a down payment of US$500 and agreed to pay US$4,000—the cost of the land—by making monthly payments of US$100 over the span of three years. They would not receive the title to their land until they made all of their payments. Instead, they received a written receipt detailing the amount they had paid and their outstanding balance.

It soon became apparent that the seller had made false promises. The city refused to provide services for this *colonia* because the land titles had not been formally registered and processed through the *ayuntamiento*. Until this process was complete, the city would not build the basic infrastructure necessary to connect the colonia to public services and refused to build public schools and parks. To complicate matters further, the city claimed that the ejido was located outside of its county line and thus the city could not be held liable for providing public services. Although Horacio had completed a small room on his property, he couldn't move in because the lack of transportation made it too difficult to get to work. To protest the conflict between the *ejidatario* and the city, which will take years to resolve, the residents of this colonia stopped making their monthly payments. Since Horacio and Mari could not move into the house they built, they gave the land to Mari's mother Clara, who continues living there.

After he stopped making payments, Horacio set aside this money toward a down payment for a house acquired through formal channels. This process would cost far more than purchasing land through the ejido, because at that time, a home loan through INFONAVIT could only be applied to a prefabricated house or apartment that was connected to public services and located near public schools and parks. By 2005, home prices had increased, ranging from US$23,000 to US$31,000. Horacio was willing to take on more debt for the type of security this loan represented. In spite of the economic insecurity generated by this debt, this loan was partly financed through the state, which meant that his land title would be legitimate and recognized by the state. Horacio would not face the same problems with the land title he faced with the ejido. In addition, Horacio wanted a physically sound structure to live in. The home he had built on his father-in-law's plot was flimsy and would not withstand a hurricane. A tour of the model home in Paseos Kabah showcased one-bedroom units painted in cheerful colors and furnished with expensive modern furniture. Horacio and Mari could readily imagine themselves living in this bright, modern abode. For these reasons, he was willing to be drawn in fully into the global finance market and to risk facing the financial chaos much of Mexico's working and middle classes experienced during the 1982 and 1994 crises.

In 2005, Horacio and Mari moved into a newly constructed, 52 square meter house in Paseos Kabah. Yet as a bartender, Horacio didn't earn enough to purchase the home outright and he had not amassed sufficient credit through INFONAVIT to purchase a house there at the price of US$23,600. Changes instituted by INFONAVIT made this possible. In 2005, INFONAVIT relaxed its rules to include tips and a spouse's income as part of worker's income, and to permit joint financing with mortgage lenders. And housing developers began building new homes that were affordable to the working class. Nonbank mortgage lenders like Hipotecaria Su Casita worked in tandem with developers like Grupo Sadasi to finance these homes. Su Casita gave Horacio a loan of Mex$64,349 (approximately US$6,400, with an interest rate of 10.59 percent) to supplement his INFONAVIT loan of Mex$166,303 and his down payment of Mex$7,347. The INFONAVIT loan was on a twenty-five-year mortgage. Initially, Horacio made monthly mortgage payments of US$150, one-fourth of which went to INFONAVIT and three-fourths to Su Casita. "I was so excited when I signed the mortgage papers," Horacio recalled. The idea of owning a brand new modern home "filled [him] with excitement" because it was a dream that he had previously considered unattainable. Horacio was proud of his new one-bedroom home because it was "modern." In contrast to his *cuartito* (small room), it has indoor plumbing, tiled floors, concrete walls and a sturdy roof, and a small yard where his daughters can play. Most importantly, the bus stop was located one block from his house.

But Horacio did not fully comprehend the terms of the bargain he made with Hipotecaria Su Casita. "They paint a pretty picture. You are over the moon when you sign the papers. I did not understand what I was signing," he said. He didn't realize that his monthly payment would increase annually or that his loan was based on compounded interest. In spite of the pleasure and security he feels in his new home, he was shocked by how much debt he accumulated within the space of a few months. Unlike the model home, his house came unfurnished, without basic trimmings like light fixtures. In addition to his monthly payments, Horacio spent his savings to make a down payment of US$1,000 and to purchase security bars for his windows and doors (US$500). To furnish his home, he opened a credit line of US$300 at a local furniture store. Considering that he earned US$400 a month (not including tips) as a hotel bartender, most of his income was allocated to pay his debt.

He and his family have taken on enormous economic insecurity. This debt makes Horacio "feel tied down to Cancún" because "you can't miss a payment or you risk losing your house. . . . It makes you work harder." To pay his debt, Horacio reduced his visits to Kuchmil and stopped sending money to his parents. He was unable to save and relied increasingly on credit to get by.

When the Great Recession hit in 2008, his careful economic balancing act began to unravel. Within seven years, he had paid Su Casita Mex$150,000 (over twice the amount of the original loan) and still owed Mex$97,700. This amount increased as the dollar fluctuated. When he purchased his home, the peso was valued at eight pesos per US dollar, but as the value of the dollar continued to escalate, Horacio went deeper into debt.

In the summer of 2011, Horacio found himself unable to keep up with his debts. The decline in tourism made it difficult for Horacio to keep pace with the cost of living in a tourist city, where the local economy is fueled by dollars, not pesos. In addition to his mortgage, he had borrowed money to buy a motorcycle, a computer, and furniture. He began selling off goods to liquidate some of his debts. He fell four months behind on his mortgage payments and was threatened with foreclosure. Su Casita faced a similar fate. After it filed for bankruptcy, its debt was purchased for pennies on the dollar by a revolving door of nonbank mortgage lenders. Each lender showed up at his door with new terms and conditions and threats of eviction for nonpayment. These tactics were outsourced to private companies that deploy teams of armed men to knock on doors, post nonpayment or eviction notices on doors, and in the most dire cases, physically force people out of their homes. Representatives of nonbank lenders denounce these strong-arm tactics, but they acknowledge that they are understaffed and cannot stop subcontracting.

To avoid losing his house, Horacio sold his car. Tourism picked up again in part due to the hype and global coverage of ancient Mayan predictions of the world ending on December 21, 2012, so he was able to get on back on track with his payments. But Horacio worries that despite this upturn he will be unable to keep up with his mortgage payments. His modern home has become an economic albatross. The mortgage lending business, he tells me, is a "big scam." Echoes of Horacio's story have been experienced throughout the Paseos Kabah neighborhood, where residents told me that two-thirds of them are going through foreclosure or have simply walked away from their homes.

Normalizing Debt

The crises I highlighted—Fox's push to help Cancún recover after a hurricane by promoting a "property-owning democracy" and the housing woes Horacio and others face—speak to the changing meanings of debt and risk in modern Mexico. The transition to a "property-owning democracy" is rooted in inclusionary and exclusionary practices rooted in settler colonial logics of improvement. As debt becomes what Susanne Soederberg refers to as "the ordinary run of things," it is leading toward greater dispossession and expropriation (2014, 166). The argument that poverty and the lack of ownership precludes dignity, coupled with the demise of land redistribution, has fueled the expansion of housing finance. INFONAVIT loans have funded the construction of one of every four homes built in Mexico.[20]

With a national deficit of close to nine million homes, President Andrés Manuel López Obrador affirmed his administration's commitment to expand home construction and home loans. In Cancún, social housing continues to drive the real estate market. Private construction firms like Grupo Sadasi have filled in the void left after the state moved away from housing construction and land redistribution. Established in 1975, Grupo Sadasi is one of the biggest housing developers in Mexico and was one of the first developers to build affordable homes in Cancún. With extensive land reserves, Sadasi plans to build thirty thousand social housing units in Cancún by 2023.[21]

Since 2001, new developers, like CADU Inmobiliaria and Vivo Grupo Inmobiliario, have emerged to compete for Cancún's housing market share. CADU Inmobiliaria, which was established in 2004, now controls 30 percent of Quintana Roo's housing market.[22] CADU builds homes for multiple markets, including affordable entry-level, middle–income, and single-family homes. Due to INFONAVIT's success, especially among low-income workers, INFONAVIT is being emulated throughout Latin America as a model for sustainable and affordable housing (Jha 2007; Stickney 2014). Indeed, mortgage securitization has become the largest market in Latin America (Soederberg 2014). Yet the public-private model being promoted is facing a recent foreclosure crisis that is a direct result of privatization. There is a high correlation between high vacancy rates and housing finance (Monkkonen 2018). With the state's retreat from protectionist policies and public subsidies, fiscal responsibility and private property have become the markers of modern citizenship in Mexico. Neoliberal actors' emphasis on individual economic autonomy through private debt forms part of a social mission to provide what Hipotecaria Su Casita called "safe and flexible solutions to secure your patrimony."

For Maya migrants in Cancún, this approach has pushed them to move away from a desire for autonomy from the state and the market to becoming more reliant on themselves and the market for economic security, which in turn led to greater economic insecurity as a result of the 2008 economic recession. Maya migrants are taking on debt, even though this practice increases economic risk. For Maya migrants, the risk involved in taking on debt is a loss of autonomy through servitude. Risk forms part of a moral framework where freedom has become inextricably tied to the individualization and financialization of life in Cancún. Yet given the declining productivity of farmwork, Maya communities have few options but to seek wage work in cities like Cancún. The experience of working and living in Cancún requires that Indigenous migrants negotiate their integration into this modernist project and its accompanying systems of global finance and credit. As sociologist Jane Zavisca points out in her work studying housing in Russia, home reform and its failure is a "cultural as well as economic phenomenon" and offers an instrumental moment to tease out how "credit," and I suggest risk, "can take on a distinctive moral valence" for both individuals and the state (2012, 7). This moral valence disciplines Indigenous peoples by normalizing debt and risk. It also fails to acknowledge the legacy of dispossession that forces Indigenous migrants to become indebted and return to servitude. Indeed, Horacio's cautionary tale provides a lens through which we can understand how shifts in social meanings and values attached to land, housing, and debt have led to a rise in social inequality and a global housing crisis.

3

After Housing Reform
Credit as the New Frontier

THE TRANSITION from a collective to a neoliberal model of individual property ownership marks a cultural shift in how migrants relate to land, money, and each other. Migrants who previously rejected debt now face the dilemma of taking on debt even at the risk of entering into a new form of *esclavitud*. This chapter examines the tensions produced by the shift from rejecting debt to embracing it. I first began research in Yucatán before the 1994 peso crisis and the implementation of NAFTA. Since then, I have witnessed the confusion and cynicism evoked by the peso revaluation, the encroachment of US-subsidized corn and the subsequent reduction in Maya farmers' earning capacity, the imposition of additional austerity measures, and the rising privatization of Mexico's industries. When I moved to Cancún in 2001 to conduct dissertation fieldwork, credit and its circulation (or lack thereof) were of central concern to migrants and their families. Without credit, they could not survive the ups and downs of a tourist economy. My own quest for housing gave me a new point of entry to understand migrants' access to credit. I rented a semifurnished two-bedroom apartment in downtown Cancún; it included two sofas built into the living room decor and a kitchen outfitted with cabinets and modern appliances, a rare occurrence in Mexico's housing market, where apartments are usually stripped bare of everything including overhead light fixtures. My shoestring student budget made it difficult to buy additional furniture, like a dining set and a bed. I turned to Kuchmil migrants, who had limited access to credit but nonetheless were savvy at finding goods and avoiding debt. They first directed me to the secondhand market because goods were sold at a fraction of the cost compared to commercial stores. *Tianguis*, the itinerant street markets held weekly at specified locations, were good places to find gently used furniture, they informed me. They asked their friends and networks if anyone was selling what I was buying, since informal channels of information and social networks provided a steady circulation of durable goods. Second, they recommended the electronics and furniture stores like Elektra, where customers could pay cash or purchase goods on credit. Migrants encouraged me to pay cash and avoid making purchases on store credit because of their stringent requirements. To be eligible for in-store credit at commercial stores, customers were required to show proof of employment and residence. Only Maya migrants employed by formal businesses and with a verifiable address could access this type of credit. Before returning to the United States, I sold or donated these goods, many of which were earmarked for friends as soon as I purchased them.

When I returned for another round of extended fieldwork in 2014, the credit landscape was radically altered. Aggressive credit marketing was now commonplace, even among the working poor. At stores and malls, credit card representatives targeted local residents, while credit card offers arrived in the mail. Microfinance banks like Compartamos and new banks like Banco Azteca peddled small loans to working-class consumers. Established in 2002 by Grupo Elektra, Banco Azteca opened eight hundred branches within Elektra stores, a national chain that served 70 percent of Mexican households (Bruhn and Love 2014). While Maya migrants remain wary of debt, they have begun to explore these new opportunities. As a result, homes now include goods purchased on this new type of credit, like computer tablets, high-definition televisions, and elegant furniture. Kuchmil migrants' shift from avoiding debt to embracing debt could be explained as an outcome of global markets flooding Mexico with cheap goods, as the transformation of peasants into an urban proletariat, or even as a reflection of a culture of consumerism spurred by homeownership. Yet these explanations do not account for the settler and gendered logics undergirding narratives of progress and development. Migrants' forays with these new forms of credit illuminate how migrants make sense of and engage with these logics. As global capital repositions migrants as a new "frontier" and exposes them to predatory lending, these financial inclusion projects compound migrants' vulnerability along race, class, and gender lines.

Embracing Progress

How migrants negotiate the dream of homeownership and Mexican modernity illustrates the stealth ways capital transforms debt into something familiar, accessible, and desirable. Various forms of resistance are needed to combat this encroachment. Maya migrants have long aspired to own, but without debt. Yet this desire has become less feasible with the financialization of Mexico's economy. A decade ago, Maya migrants had limited access to formal credit. Due to their fear of a resurging *esclavitud*, migrants limited their debt to what they could afford. They preferred to rely on informal systems of credit like *tandas* because they were based on kin and social networks. Made up of a self-selected group of trusted friends, neighbors or family members, *tandas* are rotating credit associations. *Tanda* members agree to lend each other a fixed amount of cash, at no interest, weekly for a specific period of time. In Cancún, for example, Maya migrants participated in *tandas* that ranged from 1,000 to 5,000 pesos and included an average of ten participants who made a weekly contribution for a period of two to three months. Each week the entire pot is disbursed to a member of the group until everyone has taken a turn. These funds were used to cover expenses like building a house or purchasing durable goods. In the case of self-built housing, which entails building with cash at hand, having the money to purchase durable home goods in addition to construction materials required a careful calculus that took into account ongoing construction expenses and wage fluctuations. These goods were usually purchased in cash, secondhand or through store layaway programs. Debt was perceived to lead to dispossession and thus best avoided.

Over the past decade, hotels, banks, and private developers have provided new credit opportunities for migrants. In response to the state's retreat from land subsidy programs and the devastation of Hurricane Wilma, Maya migrants have taken on debt, even though this practice increases economic risk. They have used it to purchase cars, electronics, and housing. How do Maya migrants reconcile this cultural shift? "If you wish to advance (*progresar*), [you need to] expose yourself to risk," explained Jovana, a migrant from Kuchmil. This declaration, which was repeated by other Maya migrants, contrasts sharply with migrants' prior understandings of the meanings of money and consumption. For male migrants, going into debt to purchase a home was a risky venture that ignored lessons learned from Indigenous experiences with debt peonage. For female migrants, owning a concrete block home has become a sign of both progress *and* security from natural disasters. Credit becomes a way to tap into these desires for progress, even as it places the dream of modernity at risk and severely strains social ties and reciprocal relations.

The Rise of Credit

The push toward individualized debt is an outcome of the consumer and debt policies that began in the 1970s under the Institutional Revolutionary Party (Partido Revolucionario Institucional or PRI). The end of the "Mexican Miracle," a period of economic growth that ran from the late 1940s through the late 1960s, prompted the government to adopt a debt-based growth approach to stabilize the economy (L. Walker 2013). The government subsidized growth through foreign loans by providing mortgage subsidies and consumer credit for the middle class, and by taxing goods. To protect its new consumer-citizens, it created the National Fund for Worker Consumption (Fondo Nacional para el Consumo de Trabajadores or FONACOT) in 1973 and instituted the 1976 Federal Law for the Protection of the Consumer (Ley Federal de Protección al Consumidor), making it possible for middle-class consumers to access affordable credit outside of the banking system and to prosecute merchant fraud or abuse (L. Walker 2013). In 1976, two institutions, PROFECO and the National Institute for the Consumer (Instituto Nacional del Consumidor or INCO), were created to enforce the law and inculcate new consumer habits. The onset of the 1982 debt crisis due to the loss of oil revenues and the government's defaulting on loan repayments prompted a shift—directed by the International Monetary Fund—away from state-led development toward neoliberal policies that favored debt repayment. Natural disasters like the 1985 Mexico City earthquake and Hurricane Gilbert in 1988 further exacerbated the impact of the crisis on consumers.

In contrast to the presidential administrations of Luis Echeverría (1970–76) and José López Portillo (1976–82), which enacted policies to buttress the middle class, the later administrations of Miguel de la Madrid (1982–88), Carlos Salinas de Gortari (1988–94) and Ernesto Zedillo (1994–2000) embraced a neoliberal economic model that limited state intervention, reduced public spending, privatized state institutions, and promoted free trade. This approach was intended to reduce state spending, but it led to the expansion of bank credit, placing the banking system at great economic risk. After Salinas de Gortari privatized state-owned banks in order to generate funds to cover a ballooning deficit, housing loans nearly tripled (Haber 2005). The 1994 peso collapse resulted in a major bailout to prevent the banking industry from collapsing and opened the door for foreign banks to take controlling interest of Mexico's biggest banks (ibid.). After being encouraged to take on debt, disillusioned middle-class business owners and farmers refused to pay back their loans, coalescing into a movement known as *El Barzón* (Grammont 2001). The implementation of NAFTA displaced two million farmers who could not compete with cheap American imports of corn and other produce, and promoted the privatization of *ejido* lands.[1] Escalating inflation fueled by peso devaluations and steep drops in real income led to a reduction in household spending and consumption through the 1990s. These austerity measures fomented greater economic inequality and shrank the middle class, with deleterious effects on the poor and Indigenous communities.[2] These measures have been touted as the growing pains Mexico must endure to move from the so-called Third World to the First. However, for Maya communities, the axioms of individualized debt and private land ownership underpinning these reforms echo settler colonial logics and have resulted in displacement and dispossession.

Poverty as the New Frontier

The shift toward individualized debt and the emphasis on the consumer-citizen became more pronounced under Vicente Fox's administration (2000–6). However, unlike previous policies that favored the middle class, Fox's policies were directed at the working and lower middle classes. Like Hernando de Soto, Fox envisioned the poor as an untapped source of capital and self-actualization. To make this vision a reality, Fox turned to the work of Muhammad Yunus, whom he first met in 1997 when he was governor of Guanajuato.[3] As managing director and founder of Grameen Bank in Bangladesh, Yunus is considered the pioneer of microcredit, for which he was awarded a Nobel Prize in 2006. These "credits" are short-term loans for the "unbankable"—the poor, primarily rural women, who do not have collateral and thus cannot seek out traditional bank loans.[4] Grameen Bank is premised on the model that "the poor are inherently entrepreneurial" and serves as "an example of the democratization of capital" (Roy 2010, 3). When Fox became president, he invited Yunus to help expand the microcredit industry in Mexico. Fox raved about Yunus's work:

And we look for example at Bangladesh, a poor, small country, and we find they have the best microlending system. It's a miracle. It's the best tool that I have known yet to combat poverty with dignity, [helping] people to overcome poverty by their own effort. And so we've reproduced that model now in Mexico. The microlending system is spreading throughout all Mexico and is going to empower and give capacities and opportunities to millions of women that are [so] poor today that they don't know how to read or write. [When] they take advantage of this opportunity and they overcome their poverty, [then] they start the educational [and] cultural change within themselves.[5]

If Bangladesh, an impoverished and vulnerable country according to Fox, considered its poor a worthy investment, why couldn't Mexico? With forty million people living in poverty, Mexico offered a prime opportunity to convert "dead capital" into a thriving new market (de Soto 2000). Neoliberal policies are reliant on global imaginaries and development narratives that have reconfigured the poor as a new "frontier market" for private investment (Roy 2010, 5).

Microfinance aims to alleviate poverty through "ideas of self-help and empowerment" (Roy 2010, xi). We can see this mantra at work in Fox's devotion to microfinance. For Fox, microcredits were a vehicle by which to improve the dignity of poor people's lives. "[Microcredit] dignifies," Fox stated, "because it promotes people's responsibility and people's will to work and to improve their own condition."[6] Dignity is imagined as a process that is rooted in self-actualization. As such, it is an individualizing mechanism that relies on a framework of moral uplift to justify the lack of state intervention. By helping poor women transform themselves, the state can divest itself of the responsibility to subsidize the poor. Like Yunus, Fox advocates for a social transformation that begins at home, at the level of the individual, with the hope that it will expand to the masses—especially the millions of destitute women to whom Fox alludes. Studies of microcredit caution against these expectations. Sohini Kar (2018) shows that in India, microfinance does not result in training women to be successful entrepreneurs. Microcredit may alleviate poverty, but it does not do away with it altogether (Roy 2010). It can lead to debt cycling, where borrowers use new loans to pay off previous loans (Rahman 1999). Deregulation itself creates new kinds of problems. It abets unfettered interest rates for microcredits, which can further compound poverty.

Under this model of banking on the unbanked, it is poor women and their relationships to each other that underpin the bank's financial model. Sarah Radcliffe (2015) suggests that development programs that promote microfinance and reproductive health programs rely on a neoliberal governmentality that reproduces colonial narratives of difference. "[T]hrough its structure and expectations," she explains, these programs "reproduce postcolonial expectations about ethnic communities' social cohesion, the existence of traditional communal authorities, and the docile, predictable behavior of married women, who make up the majority of credit recipients" (70). Rather than self-actualization, what takes place is a reinscription of a colonial biopolitics rooted in epistemic violence.

In addition, the language of dignity occludes the settler logic of dispossession through predation that is a hallmark of free market ideologies. When discussing the challenges of developing a microfinance industry in Mexico, Fox acknowledged the ties between deregulation and microfinance:

> Red tape is all over the system, and is yet on the system. We have to work strongly on that. We have to deregulate. We have to end red tape and we have to give all the facilities and all the flexibility [to] entrepreneurial efforts, and this is part of the things that we are trying to accomplish. Unfortunately we have a cultural paternalism here in Mexico. You don't see the reaction of entrepreneurship that we would like to [have], pushing and opening up new businesses all over Mexico.[7]

Paternalistic models of governance that were emblematic of PRI administrations are considered anachronistic to financial instruments of global finance. An unfettered state—a neoliberal mantra—is essential for microfinance and dispossession to thrive.

Gendering Risk

In 2014, Fátima, a thirty-three-year-old migrant from Kuchmil, took out a microfinance loan with her circle of friends and neighbors. I have known Fátima since she was six years old. At that tender age, Fátima became my unofficial "chaperone" in Kuchmil. She shadowed me on visits to meet local families and accompanied me on bicycle treks to neighboring villages. When I lived in Cancún in 2014, she babysat my children on occasion. One afternoon as we observed our children playing together in the shade of the enclosed patio of her home, she explained that the money she received for babysitting would allow her to pay down her debt. "What debt?" I prompted. "I have taken out a *crédito* (loan) with a group of women," explained Fátima. As a stay-at-home mother, Fátima didn't have direct access to formal credit like bank loans and store credit. For the working class, checking and savings accounts are provided through an employer. With the rise of homeownership in Mexico, as in the United States after World War II, there has been a concomitant rise in consumerism, which requires greater access to credit.[8]

"Is it a *tanda*?" I ask Fátima about the loan. The *tanda* is a common method by which migrants save money. Fátima's *crédito* wasn't a *tanda* but it was structured like one: a group of thirteen women who trusted each other pooling money together. Unlike the *tandas* Fátima had joined in the past where the pot of money came from participants' savings or salaries, the *crédito* was funded by the Crédito Mujer program of Compartamos Bank (Compartamos Banco). Crédito Mujer provides short-term microfinance loans (ranging between Mex$1,500 and Mex$27,000) for women organized into groups of at minimum ten members to start or expand a small business; they are paid back over a period of sixteen weeks. Members are encouraged to save a small sum each week, which gets deposited in a bank account and disbursed back to each member after the loan has been paid. The loans are disbursed to the individuals at the beginning of the payment period, but repayment is a collective process that relies on peer pressure to reduce defaulting on the loan. Interest rates are not regulated for these types of lenders; the annual interest rate for Crédito Mujer was 71.2 percent.[9] The group elected a committee, consisting of a president and treasurer, whose responsibility was to collect weekly payments and deposit this money in the bank. After each successful loan cycle, the group was invited to request another loan and granted a higher credit limit. The first time Fátima participated in Crédito Mujer, her group received individual loans of 2,500 pesos. The second time the group was granted individual loans of 4,000 pesos.

I asked Fátima about the business she was funding with the loan. I knew she cut hair on occasion and wondered if this was the business she planned to fund. "The *crédito* was intended for a business but I used it to pay a debt," Fátima explained. "What about the other women?" I inquired. "Some of them had businesses. One bought merchandise for her store. Another sold shoes. Another sold cosmetics. The others used it pay their debts too." Fátima considered the weekly contributions to be manageable. For the first loan, each member paid two hundred pesos weekly; in addition, members contributed to a savings account and each paid eleven additional pesos weekly to cover the taxi ride for the treasurer, who made the weekly deposits. Fátima set aside thirty pesos weekly for this savings fund. For the second loan, each member paid 350 pesos weekly, in addition to the eleven pesos for the taxi and money allocated for savings. Since Fátima joined forces with her brother to save during the second round, she contributed an additional 225 pesos weekly toward savings.

For Indigenous women like Fátima, credit was not empowering. Instead, it became a debilitating process. Things went awry soon after receiving the first line of credit, when one member soon began to miss payments. The other members covered the missing contributions with money from their savings. Failure to do so would place their collateral at risk. Crédito Mujer does not officially require collateral, but Fátima's group was required to sign a legal contract agreeing to pay back the loan. This demand reveals another level of predation, where officials contrive an additional layer of "rules" to ensnare the poor and potentially line their own pockets. The contract made Fátima nervous. "With this contract, they can take your house and there are people who have lost their car as a result. At least that's what our group was told." The group worried they would be unable to keep up with the payments and would face the potential loss of their homes. The group was able to avoid defaulting on their loan, but to do so, they had to forsake their savings, at great hardship to themselves and their families. Fátima lost six hundred pesos with the first loan cycle. Her husband advised her not to join another group. "You are not going to join Compartamos," he proclaimed. "It's a waste if you are saving and someone stops making their payments. You aren't working. It's not right that they take away your money." Fátima concurred, but she rejoined the Compartamos group when her sister urged her to do so because they were short one member and after her brother agreed to help her pay the loan. Like with the first line of credit, the treasurer—the same person who failed to pay her loan previously—stopped making payments around the eighth week of the payment schedule, but the treasurer was able to cover the payments with the money she had saved. Things fell apart during the very last meeting. Fátima arrived late because she had been busy picking up her children from school. The group was wrapping up when they informed Fátima that her savings had been used to cover a deficit. "The treasurer who was supposed to deposit the payments did not do so for the last three payments. She spent it. Since her husband was a taxi driver, he would take her to make the deposits. But they stopped making the deposits. When I arrived, the group had disbursed each member's savings. I had saved

3,600 pesos. They used my savings to replace the missing funds. All my savings were gone." In this instance the risk was not spread equally among the group as had been the case for the previous loan; Fátima was the only one who lost all of her savings. "They were supposed to take money from each person, but because I saved the most, they took all of my money." The treasurer justified her behavior by explaining that her husband had left her. "They had problems," explained Fátima. "We went as a group to her house. She told me she didn't have any money to pay the debt. To this day she has not paid me back."

This system of finance relies on peer monitoring to reduce the moral hazard of loan defaults. What was intended to stimulate entrepreneurship and promote economic stability resulted in creating greater economic precarity for these women and straining social relations. While Compartamos literally translates into the declarative statement "We share," poor women bear the bulk of the financial burden. As Fátima explained, "The bank doesn't lose." Should they default on their loan, members jeopardize more than their financial well-being. They also risk severely damaging their personal relationships and social networks as they forge new ways of relating to money and debt. Fátima felt betrayed by the group, even by her sister, who explained she was outvoted by the group on how best to replace the stolen funds. "The terrible thing about the group was that they didn't behave in solidarity with me. In fact that's what it's called, 'a solidarity group, that's how we share,' how we help each other." Fátima believes the group placed their self-interests ahead of hers. "The women wanted to keep borrowing money. They decided that they could pay the bank with my savings and they would remain clean. They wouldn't be reported to the credit bureau and could keep asking for more loans." Fátima's brother was furious to have lost his money, but he didn't blame Fátima for the group's decision. He did pressure Fátima to recoup his money, but the treasurer became increasingly hostile after each confrontation. They never recouped their money. Traumatized by this experience, Fátima refused to join another group and has become wary of microfinance. But this does not mean that she eschews credit. "Next time we need a loan, it's best if we turn to BanCoppel," she explained. With the advent of banks like BanCoppel that offer personal loans at similar rates to Compartamos, she has other options. Fátima's story illuminates how gender, race, and class intersect to produce financial beings and construct a new financial landscape in Mexico. As microcredit strains trusted social networks, if not severing them altogether, Maya migrants find themselves being pushed to turn away from each other. For some, this may mean greater isolation as they immerse themselves in the individualization promoted by financial inclusion programs. Others interpret these experiences as reminders that social ties matter and will provide a buffer in an economic system where indebtedness has become the norm.

Fátima's participation in Crédito Mujer is inextricably tied to the rise of a global microfinance industry. Established as a nonprofit microlending bank in 1990, Compartamos Banco was converted into a for-profit commercial bank on April 20, 2007. Its Initial Public Offering (IPO) transformed Compartamos into the largest microfinance bank in Latin America, with a gross loan portfolio of US$1.2 million.[10] Fátima's story reminds us that these new systems of global finance are gendered. When microfinance was introduced to Latin America, it did not initially target women. However, Grameen Bank's success with women entrepreneurs popularized microfinance as a vehicle for "female empowerment." Ninety percent of Compartamos clientele are women.[11] They are targeted through door-to-door promotions, radio ads, promotional events, and fliers.[12] As Melanie Moodie explains, microfinance "exploit[s] and amplif[ies]" gendered difference in order to code this enterprise as feminine (2013, 283). Whereas "microfinance is always already coded as feminine by virtue of its scale (micro, small, domestic), activities (reproductive), and relationship to peril" (290), global capitalism is gendered masculine through its representational practices, through the social norms of investment bank culture, and through discursive practices that divorce the world of finance from feminized reproductive labor. The infiltration of microfinance in Mexico entails more than the introduction of poor women to new financial instruments. Individual, personal debt is launched into the realm of high-risk finance with its discourses on peril and value. "Global discourses of risk," Moodie argues, "are gendered such that a particular set of financial investment strategies (also known as casino or frontier capitalism) are coded as masculine in relation to this feminized, often invisible, reproductive labor" (2013, 280). Migrants' participation in microfinance illuminates how risk is gendered, but it also shows how credit takes on a "moral valence" that is rooted in personal relationships (Zavisca 2012, 7).

Gender difference, however, is not the only trope at play in Fátima's willingness to embrace debt even when perpetual indebtedness looms large. Since gender, racial, and class subordination work simultaneously to disenfranchise Indigenous peoples, an intersectional analysis is critical for understanding dispossession and combating settler and (neo)colonial impositions (Barker 2017; Crenshaw 1991; Radcliffe 2015; Ramirez 2007b). Indeed, microfinance banks are not just fixated on poor women in Cancún. They also target poor *Indigenous* women. This process prompts us to consider not just the "gender of risk," as Moodie suggests, but how debt, with all its associated risks, is made desirable for Indigenous people. The *tanda*-inspired model of banking represents an example of how culturally salient organizing practices are adapted to draw Indigenous people into new modes of finance. But there is more at stake here than convincing Indigenous people to borrow money. Just as finance is organized around gendered representational practices, it is also predicated on settler colonial and colonial logics. Sarah Radcliffe (2015) shows how development policies implemented in Ecuador rely on social categories that remain rooted in colonial representations of Indigenous women as docile bodies. As a result, these policies fail to improve Indigenous women's lives, instead marginalizing and excluding them from leadership positions.

Indeed, global capitalism is rife with narratives of discovery. Since capitalist expansion demands new zones of extraction, the emergence of "resource frontiers"—spaces that are deregulated to promote resource extraction, be they rainforests, rivers, or Indigenous pueblos—form part of a history of European colonialism (Tsing 2005). The language of "new markets" and "frontier capitalism" evokes settler colonial logics that convert Indigenous peoples and their lands into likely targets for dispossession. In Latin America, the recent proliferation of financial instruments, like microfinance, credit cards, and mortgages, is designed to attract sectors of the population previously excluded from financial markets, in this case poor women and working-class families. Progress, they are told, demands risk. The language of capital not only genders risk, it imagines new virtual and physical terrains for discovery, settlement, and profit. The virtual is embodied in new instruments (e.g., mortgages and credit cards) and new markets (e.g., real estate), while the physical is captured by the landscape (the expropriation of ejido lands) and Indigenous women (new consumers). In Cancún, the housing and consumer boom are an outcome of these twin logics of discovery and dispossession. Tourists are invited to discover Maya culture, while Indigenous migrants are encouraged to buy into the settler dream of homeownership and modern consumerism, repositioning poor women and Indigenous migrants as the new "frontier" for development.

Unfettering Credit

Under neoliberalism in Mexico, debt is the outcome of poverty as the new frontier. As social programs came to see homeownership as a path out of poverty, the consumer-citizen became a new market. Homeownership, through the expansion of social housing, has come to serve a similar function as it does in the United States, as an engine for consumer spending (Cohen 2003). This outcome was calculated. After World War II, Nancy Kwak (2015) shows, American housing experts and advisors sought to naturalize mass homeownership and consumption globally, making homeownership "a tool of foreign policy and . . . a vehicle for international development" (8). Not surprisingly, marketing campaigns for social housing borrowed the familiar trope of suburban domesticity central to US real estate markets. Oriented around the triad of consumer culture, homeownership, and the nuclear family, suburban domesticity was a powerful tool to contain threats to national ideals and unruly subjects, and to promote capitalism and a liberal democracy (May 1988).

In Mexico, advertisements, from billboards to brochures, display images of modern landscaped homes and happy nuclear families. The majority of these ads feature families with European or Anglo features, but occasionally the advertisements targeting working-class families include families with brown skin. Grupo Sadasi's marketing campaigns for their new Prado Norte development plays up the dream of homeownership. The 2014 campaign states:"You live well. And yes, you can afford it!"as a young girl with brown skin jumps for joy in front of her new house (fig. 4). This theme was carried forward in their 2019 marketing slogan as "*¿Antojo de vivir mejor? Tenemos el lugar perfecto.*" (Do you desire to live better? We have the perfect place). This campaign depicts life in Prado Norte as the good life:

> Es el mejor conjunto habitacional de su tipo en Cancún, un lugar seguro para ti y tu familia. Desarrollo integral con casas de 2 recámaras, todos los servicios y en una zona de gran plusvalía al norponiente de la Ciudad.
>
> ¡¡¡En Prado Norte los sueños que has tenido se hacen realidad!!!
>
> Prado Norte, ha sido desarrollado pensando en el bienestar de todos sus residentes; a través de un estilo de vida diferente.[13]

> (It's the best housing complex of its type in Cancún, a safe place for you and your family. Integrated development includes homes with two bedrooms, utility services included, and located in an up-and-coming zone northwest of the City.

FIGURE 4. Prado Norte "You live well" campaign. Photograph by author.

In Prado Norte, all your dreams will become a reality!!!
Prado Norte has been planned for the well-being of all its residents;
based on a different lifestyle.)

The emphasis on a "different lifestyle" is central to social housing campaigns. In a country where self-built housing, until recently, constituted 74 percent of the total housing stock (PUEC-UNAM 2013), convincing people to buy a prefabricated home for a princely sum takes amazing sleight of hand. Narratives of the good life and images of modern amenities and stylish comfort form part of these deft maneuvers. Model homes are decorated with vibrant colors and artfully displayed with chic modern furniture. This staging echoes the architectural precision of American suburbia and thus invokes the familiar narrative of the American dream. This narrative of the good life is evoked in advertisements for housing projects targeting the middle and upper classes in Cancún (fig. 5). The message is clear to any buyer. The good life entails more than just a house; this house must be filled with goods. Yet acquiring these goods necessitates becoming enmeshed with another instrument of finance—the credit card. The home becomes the vessel through which credit—and debt—become essential to living this dream.

FIGURE 5. Condominium under construction with sign "Welcome to your new life." Photograph by author.

Consumer spending in Mexico has been hampered by limited credit access and high interest rates. Banco Azteca was the first bank to target the poor for potential investment and growth. In 2002, Banco Azteca expanded its credit services; in addition to its consumer loan for in-store purchases at Elektra stores, it now offers a store credit card (Tarjeta Azteca Visa) and personal loans.[14] Nevertheless, credit card rates remain volatile and exorbitant, due to a fluctuating currency, limited competition, and lax regulation and oversight (OECD 2004). For first-time borrowers and low-income consumers, rates and fees, for example, can go up to 88 percent for a credit card from BanCoppel.[15] Despite efforts to expand access to financial services, at least half of Mexicans did not have a credit card or bank account in 2012 (Reddy, Bruhn, and Tan 2013). Only 29 percent of Mexicans had a credit card account by 2015 (ENIF 2015). Likewise, credit card spending has grown incrementally, increasing from 0.59 percent of national spending in 2001 to 2.38 percent in 2007.[16] Mexico's domestic credit spending has continued to remain low, constituting 31.1 percent of the gross national product in 2016.[17] According to the statistics of the most recent financial inclusion survey published by the National Banking and Securities Commission (Comisión Nacional Bancaria y de Valores or CNBV), only 47 percent of Mexico's population has an account with a financial institution (De Noriega Olea, Sakar Almirante, and Romero Sotelo 2019).

This gap has become an opportunity to advocate for the "financial inclusion" of the working class. In 2006, the Mexican government prioritized financial education (Reddy et al. 2013). With support from the World Bank, the Mexican government designed and implemented a National Financial Inclusion Strategy, a comprehensive plan that brings together private banking, social welfare, education, and telecommunications to bolster access to financial services.[18] The World Bank also developed several projects to expand credit in Mexico. The US$100 million Savings and Credit Sector Consolidation and Financial Inclusion Project targeted the improvement and consolidation of savings and credit institutions for the benefit of women and Indigenous communities in rural areas.[19] The US$400 million Expanding Rural Finance program expanded credit for rural micro, small, and medium enterprises, the majority of which are female owned.[20] Through its private sector arm, the IFC, the World Bank funded the development of microfinance banks like Compartamos, Progresemos, and Camesa.[21] The López Obrador administration is following suit by building the telecommunications infrastructure necessary to expand financial services in rural areas.[22] As the unbanked are refashioned into monetized subjects, they have become a rich resource to tap, like oil and tourism, in the name of Mexican modernity.

The Credit Card Workshop

Conversations on housing in Cancún inevitably turned to stories about consumption and credit when I lived there. "Can you explain how credit cards work?" Miguel, a Kuchmil migrant, asked me after he shared his story of his INFONAVIT loan. Miguel was tempted by the proliferation of credit offers, accompanied by smooth sales pitches, at stores and via television and other media. Unfamiliar with credit cards, Miguel paid attention to his friends' credit card woes. One friend had taken out a credit card knowing he was unable to pay back his debt. "What happened to him?" I ask. "He figures they won't be able to find him because he switched addresses." Another friend received a credit card offer from his bank by mail. He ignored the request, only to find that credit card fees were being deducted from his savings account. When he spoke to a bank representative, he was informed that the account would remain open until he made a formal request to close it. The fees were standard operating fees that accumulated regardless if he used the card or not. These stories of chicanery and dishonesty made Miguel hesitant to open a credit card account. Migrants turned to me to parse out what was true and false because I spent my days meeting with directors of government agencies like CONDUSEF.

To avoid compounding this sense of confusion, I paired up with PROFECO to offer an informational workshop on credit cards. PROFECO was established in 1976 to protect consumer rights and promote responsible consumption. To that end, the agency's education division in Cancún provides workshops in situ on consumer rights. When I explained to Lic. Jazmín Garnica Ortiz, head of that division, that Maya migrants didn't have time to take the twelve-week course offered by her office, she agreed to consider alternative ways to grant them access to this information. If I were willing to organize a workshop, she offered to recommend a *promotora* from her office who, for a small fee, could facilitate the workshop. I reached out to Maya migrants for recommendations of places to hold the workshop and potential catering services. They proposed I rent a hall located near Paseos Kabah and encouraged me to provide a hearty meal. Most migrants have very little time off from work, usually one day a week; providing a meal was one way to compensate them for their time. I was given the name of a vendor who sold *cochinita pibil*, a marinated pork stew. Migrants from Kuchmil who lived in Paseos Kabah and the *regiones* neighboring this *fraccionamiento*, and residents who participated in a housing survey I conducted in Paseos Kabah were invited to the workshop. The open air hall, typically used to celebrate weddings, was spacious and included round tables and chairs. To accommodate the promotora's schedule, the two-hour workshop was held on a Saturday morning. In spite of these efforts, only eight people were able to attend the workshop. Only one man was present, but it was not Miguel, who had to work that day. The rest of the participants were women who brought their children, ranging from toddlers to teenagers. The older children were corralled into babysitting the younger ones. Six of the participants were from Kuchmil, while the other two were mestizas who lived in Paseos Kabah.

The promotora began the workshop by explaining the difference between PROFECO and CONDUSEF. While both agencies defend consumer rights, PROFECO protects consumers and their rights, whereas CONDUSEF protects and defends consumers of financial services. The first hour was focused on a detailed overview of how credit cards function. The second hour was focused on questions. At first the questions focused on strategies for managing credit cards, from saving receipts to double-checking that purchases matched receipts. But then the focus shifted to the theme of redress and dispossession. If PROFECO protects consumers against fraud, Pricila (a mestiza from Paseos Kabah) asked, then could they help with housing fraud? She explained that the floor of her house was cracking because the house was built over a *cenote* (sinkhole), which was now visible through the patio floor. The promotora informed the participants that PROFECO does get involved with faulty construction discovered within the warranty period. Beyond that period, the promotora encouraged them to seek help from CONDUSEF and INFONAVIT. "But when INFONAVIT became involved, that's when everything became even more difficult," Pricila explained. This observation prompted everyone to share stories of their foreclosure proceedings, of how agencies like INFONAVIT and CONDUSEF and housing developers Hipotecaria Su Casita refused to step in to resolve disputes, even when the client is unemployed and unable to pay the mortgage. Instead, INFONAVIT and Su Casita contracted collection agencies and the judicial police to bully clients into paying their debt or abandoning their homes. The next chapter focuses on these experiences.

The workshop illustrates that, for Maya migrants, credit cards cannot be disassociated from mortgages and dispossession. Credit cards represent another form of indebtedness. Because credit cards have become ubiquitous after housing reform, migrants are just as wary of these new types of debts as they were of their past incarnations. Distinguishing between credit, microfinance, and bank loans becomes a challenge when corporations like Coppel have branched out from retail and moved into banking. BanCoppel offers all types of loans, from personal to credit cards, and has become one of the biggest lenders in Mexico. Migrants like Fátima and Miguel recognize that these new forms of credit are becoming embedded in their daily lives and have the potential to become a resource during times of economic crisis. Educating themselves about credit cards is one way to mitigate, if not resist, the allure of the settler dream.

The New Credit Landscape

The push toward individualized debt has been couched behind the language of dignity and empowerment. By promoting financial inclusion, the government argues, Indigenous people, especially women, will have greater opportunity to create economic stability for themselves, their families, and their communities. Yet as Maya migrants note, individualized debt has become an extant condition that cannot be divorced from a history of *esclavitud*. This association unmasks the settler colonial logics at the heart of neoliberal endeavors to bolster entrepreneurship and homeownership among the working poor. Capitalism may look toward the poor as a new frontier. But creating new financial beings is a complicated process that reifies race, class, and gender differences, making Indigenous peoples increasingly vulnerable. Even as Maya migrants acknowledge that debt is inextricably tied to modernity, they endeavor to resist and challenge the settler logics of dispossession by evoking history and participating in collective action.

4

Foreclosure
Waiting Out the State

FORECLOSURES TAKE TIME. In Paseos Kabah, they have become a process of waiting, for paperwork to be filed, for suits and countersuits, for companies to go bankrupt and new companies to make claims, for threats of violence broadcast weekly, occasionally daily. Javier Auyero points out that "acts of waiting" are "temporal processes in and through which political subordination is produced" (2012, 2). Acts of waiting discipline citizens and illuminate the petty bureaucracy of the state and global capital. Yet they can also encourage political insubordination to take root, cultivate, and flourish (Scott 1985). Through a focus on one Maya family's experience with foreclosure, this chapter examines how diverse tactics are stitched together, from foot dragging to lawsuits, even under circumstances that make it impossible to ultimately avert eviction. In circumventing the state and private capital, Maya migrants constitute what Asef Bayat (2000) calls a "politics of redress." As Bayat notes, there are different types of resistance, not all of which result in public protest, especially under repressive regimes. A politics of redress emerges in response to state repression and seeks to carve out autonomy for the poor. In the case of Mexico, where state repression has become commonplace enough to be masked by attempts at democratization, everyday acts of resistance do not always manifest themselves in public dissent.[1] Opposition can erupt amid mundane encounters. It can transpire when the act of waiting is transformed into a process I refer to as "waiting out" the state and capital. By "waiting out" INFONAVIT and mortgage companies, Maya migrants sidestep the bureaucratic measures created to regulate the poor and manufacture consent and convert them into provocative acts of obstruction and defiance. I examine how the temporality of "waiting out" subverts indeterminate waiting as a mode of political domination.

This chapter also considers the way foreclosure narrates belonging in contemporary Mexico. In the popular imaginary, Indigenous people are associated with land, but not with homeownership.[2] But as Indigenous people enter real estate markets and become homeowners, they are exposed to predatory lending and become susceptible to the risk of foreclosure. In this context, foreclosure makes evident that neoliberal policies promoting privatization of land and the environment are entwined with Indigenous dispossession. How do Indigenous peoples cope with dispossession, and how does this loss (re)structure their attachments to place, land, and nation? How is this violence gendered and racialized? Housing reform and foreclosure become a form of discipline to produce new types of citizens and construct new narratives of progress, debt delinquency, and insecurity. In spite of these disciplinary tactics, Maya migrants' resistance strategies, from hiring lawyers to forming grassroots political organizations, help construct solidarity and new forms of social agency and redress through the process of waiting out the state. These mobilizations, insurgent practices, and everyday encroachments help us reimagine the political and the meanings of citizenship for Indigenous communities within the context of urban and tourist economies (e.g., Bayat 2010; Holston 2008; Murphy 2015).

A Dream Forestalled

"We have a good ten years before we lose our house," Mariela and Francisco remarked upon their foreclosure proceedings. A decade marks more than just the loss of a house. It captures the end of a dream of homeownership and the beginning of a new form of *esclavitud*, of debt pegged to a fluctuating dollar in an economy in freefall. It is punctuated by episodic failures of petty capitalism embarked upon to avert this fate. It evinces the temporality of waiting out capital and the state. This chapter follows Mariela and Francisco's efforts to convert time into an act of defiance and resistance by drawing on a history of Indigenous resistance.

Mariela and Francisco were among the first Kuchmil migrants to purchase a home in a housing development. They were able to do so because they had spent a decade working in Cancún. Francisco first began doing menial jobs in hotels and eventually earned a position as a waiter. When he first arrived in Cancún, he rented a room with his older brother. After his brother purchased a lot that included a one-room concrete block house and was previously owned by their aunt through a *traspaso* (transfer), he invited Francisco to move in with him. His brother built two rooms behind the house that he rented to friends and family members. When Francisco married Mariela, they rented one of these rooms. Mariela worked as a domestic servant in a private home for a middle-class Mexican family. Prior to getting married, she had lived with her younger sister and brother-in-law and their child in a small three-room apartment. Mariela and Francisco didn't plan to rent for long and began searching for affordable plots of land. They had some savings set aside.

When they initiated their search, they learned of the new affordable houses in Paseos Kabah. Mariela and Francisco were attracted to the dream of owning a modern prefabricated home. Yet, in light of Maya people's history with debt peonage, Maya migrants have long been resistant to taking on debt. Mariela and Francisco overcame their hesitation because their options were limited. Their full-time jobs prevented them from lobbying for land from the state, the typical method by which migrants procured affordable land tracts. Purchasing a home through Cancún's real estate market was cost prohibitive. The new housing developments, however, filled this gap by giving working-class and lower-middle-class Cancunenses access to affordable housing. Social housing seemed a provident and prudent way to fulfill the dream of homeownership, even it if meant going into debt.

Mariela and Francisco chose Paseos Kabah, one of the first social housing developments built in Cancún after housing reform, because the two-story model had greater potential for expandability. While they did not have children at the time, they eagerly anticipated a future filled with children. Since they were both employed full-time, social housing appeared to be an affordable choice. Although Francisco was eligible for an INFONAVIT credit, his salary base was insufficient to earn enough points to qualify for a home loan substantial enough to purchase one of the newly constructed houses in Paseos Kabah. These homes were priced at approximately US$23,000.[3] INFONAVIT provided Francisco with a loan for Mex$91,000. To make up the difference, Francisco paired this loan with a Mex$79,000 loan from the private mortgage company Hipotecaria Su Casita. This loan consisted of an adjustable rate pegged to the dollar, not the peso. At this point in time, one dollar was equivalent to eight pesos. Pegging the loan to the dollar was not surprising, since the government had a history of inducing Mexican firms to authorize debt contracts in dollars and created the Unit of Account (Unidad de Inversión or UDI) system to protect bank stockholders from inflation (Haber 2005).[4]

After purchasing their home, Mariela and Francisco carefully planned its expansion. Social housing comes with few amenities. The original house included a basic floor plan (72 square meters). The first floor included one large room encompassing the living room and kitchen, a bathroom, and a bedroom. A second bedroom was located upstairs on the second floor. Units lack light fixtures, kitchen appliances, and window protectors. A small counter with a sink separated the kitchen area from the living area. The lack of windows kept the sunlight out but the heat in. Windows were located in the front and back walls, but the shared side walls had no windows. To make the space comfortable and functional, Mariela and Francisco dreamed of converting the first-floor bedroom into an airy kitchen. To do so entailed moving a bedroom to the second floor and building over much of the small patio located behind the unit. It took them a few years to make these additions, because they purchased construction materials bit by bit, paying for all renovations in cash. They kept costs low by hiring a cousin from Kuchmil who spent a few weeks each year on these projects.

The kitchen renovations were completed before health ailments and changes in the economy ended up derailing their plans. A few years after they purchased their home, Francisco developed an autoimmune disorder, which was further compounded by the onset of diabetes. Plagued by poor health, Francisco reduced his working hours for a couple of years. To make up for his lost wages, Mariela worked seven days a week. As a result, adding a second bedroom upstairs took time. In spite of these challenges, Francisco continued making mortgage payments to Hipotecaria Su Casita. The INFONAVIT loan was manageable because it was set at a fixed rate and was garnished from Francisco's wages. However, when the Great Recession reduced tourist visits to Cancún, workers like Francisco were hard hit. Fewer tourists meant reduced tips for service workers. Waiters like Francisco depend on tips for at least half of their income. To account for fluctuations in a tourist economy that is dependent on seasonal tourism, migrants typically save money during the peak season to carry them through the low periods. Despite these efforts, Mariela and Francisco's small savings could not cushion them from the rippling effects of a global recession and an unanticipated health crisis.

Averting Bankruptcy

The Great Recession was precipitated by the US mortgage industry crisis, but it had a domino effect that burst housing bubbles in countries like Spain. Spain's banks were heavily invested in the housing market, not just locally, but globally.[5] The semipublic Spanish savings-and-loans bank Caja Madrid owned 40 percent of Hipotecaria Su Casita in 2010. After the housing bubble burst, property developers went bankrupt, leaving *cajas*, regional savings banks, holding their debts (López and Rodríguez 2011). To prevent their collapse, seven *cajas* (Caja Madrid, Bancaja, La Caja de Canarias, Caja de Ávila, Caixa Laietana, Caja Segovia, and Caja Rioja) were consolidated to create Bankia in December 2010. Caja Madrid held the controlling interest in this banking conglomerate. Due to its size and its heavy investment in the housing market, the Spanish government considered Bankia "too big to fail." To prevent this outcome, the government nationalized Bankia in 2012. When Su Casita collapsed soon after the global housing crash, Caja Madrid infused the private mortgage lender with cash, but its own pending financial collapse made it impossible to save Su Casita.[6] As Mexico's largest nonbank mortgage and construction lender within a housing industry that is backed by the Mexican state, Su Casita was able to turn to the Mexican government to avoid declaring bankruptcy (Soederberg 2014). In September 2010, Su Casita negotiated a debt restructuring agreement with the Federal Mortgage Society (Sociedad Hipotecaria Federal or SHF), a government bank dedicated to the mortgage lending market and the promotion of social housing. This intervention postponed Su Casita's bankruptcy but did not prevent it.

While the Mexican government intervened to bail out Su Casita, it did not offer the same courtesy to the lender's clients, even though many of these clients had paired their Su Casita loan with INFONAVIT loans. In December 2010, Su Casita informed its clients that they would continue to collect mortgage payments during the debt restructuring.[7] Despite insolvency, Su Casita expected its clients to keep up with their payments and avoid insolvency themselves. However, clients like Francisco recognized the hypocrisy of this request and questioned the merit of making payments to a company that was being dismantled. Francisco's health problems and the downturn in the tourism industry were already making it difficult for Francisco to keep up with his mortgage payments. The media circus surrounding Su Casita's bankruptcy and debt restructuring proceedings left many homeowners confused about who owned their loans. In response to queries by homeowners, loan officers provided differing explanations for the outcome of the restructuring proceedings. Homeowners were told that any gap in payments would lead to immediate foreclosure. Others were told that the company would be dismantled or sold, and thus contracts with homeowners would be severed and would need to be renegotiated with the company who purchased the debt. The residents of Paseos Kabah circulated rumors and facts about what they heard, provoking further confusion over how best to proceed with mortgage payments.

Mariela and Francisco feared that Su Casita's bankruptcy or the selling off of company assets would change the terms of their loan. Since they were already behind on their payments, they assumed they would be required to renegotiate the terms of their loans with the new company. Why pay a mortgage that would be renegotiated? This assumption was based on their knowledge and experience with INFONAVIT loans. INFONAVIT has a history of negotiating repayment plans to bring delinquent clients up to date. Mariela and Francisco were proved correct. In 2011, the mortgage company Patrimonio Hipotecaria, through its subsidiary Tertius, took over collecting debt payments from Su Casita loan holders. At first, the company identified itself as Patrimonio. A year later, it identified itself as Tertius. The shifting names further confused consumers, who pondered which company they were obligated to pay: Hipotecaria Su Casita? Patrimonio? Tertius?

Patrimonio Hipotecaria was founded in 1994. Like Hipotecaria Su Casita, Patrimonio Hipotecaria was a SOFOL, a niche lender that was limited to offering credit for the housing market (Soederberg 2014). As such, it did not have the authority to purchase debts auctioned off by Su Casita. To do so, in 2010, Patrimonio established Tertius, a financial company that offers multiple forms of credit via Financial Societies of Multiple Scope (Sociedades Financieras de Objeto Múltiple or SOFOM). Although Tertius manages Patrimonios's loan portfolio, it was originally established to manage the loan portfolios of third companies purchased by Patrimonio. When Su Casita, Crédito Inmobiliario, and Hipotecaria Vértice declared bankruptcy, Tertius took over management of their loan portfolios. In 2012, Tertius began administering construction loans.[8] This is how Tertius came to collect payment on Su Casita loans.

According to Mariela and Francisco, Tertius did not contact clients in Cancún until two years after Su Casita declared bankruptcy and began restructuring its debt. They issued a new payment plan to each client. With each new owner, the terms of the loan appeared to shift, while the loan continued to grow exponentially. The adjustable rate was tied to the UDI, an indexed accounting unit pegged to the dollar and controlled by the Mexican government (Haber 2005). Between 2000 and 2010, UDI rates jumped up to 70 percent.[9] Francisco's loan was initially pegged to the exchange rate of eight pesos to the US dollar, but by 2015, the peso had jumped to fifteen pesos per dollar, doubling his loan payments. For clients who stopped paying their loans, like Francisco, the loan payments demanded by Tertius were astronomical because they included back payments and took into account the rise in the dollar's value. The initial confusion instigated by the period of waiting for the restructuring to be completed was quickly transformed into a fear of impending foreclosure.

A History of Foreclosure

Legal scholar K-Sue Park (2016) reminds us that Indigenous dispossession is the bedrock behind the expansion of American capitalism. Park traces the origins and history of the present-day mortgage instrument to early colonial America. She explains that the colonists took advantage of the divergent ways that settlers and Native Americans understood money and land. For Native Americans, money and land were not fungible commodities. Rather, land was inalienable, while "money" was vested in personal and kin relations, and its circulation was circumscribed by local markets. Mortgage foreclosure, an instrument imported from England, was reconfigured and popularized in the colonies with the intent of seizing Indigenous lands. In England, land was vested in a system of inheritance that gave preferential treatment to heirs over creditors, curtailing dispossession through foreclosure (Priest 2006); whereas in the American colonies, colonists revolutionized the British system of land entailment by making land alienable. This legal transformation made it possible for colonists to use the courts to divest Indigenous peoples of land in exchange for debt payments. Park (2016) suggests that foreclosure in colonial America became more than a set of legal practices for dispossession. It was also solidified into discursive practices to "narrat[e] history in a way that marginalizes these material processes" (Park 2016, 1008). By erasing Indigenous peoples' claims to land, foreclosure became a way to write them out of history, to solidify what Jean O'Brien (2010) calls settler "firsting" claims that constructed national histories and imaginaries devoid of Indians.

A focus on present-day foreclosure tactics attends to the ways Indigenous migrants connect these practices to a history of loss that began with colonialism. As Sarita See concludes, foreclosure is "another form of enclosure" because it divests the subprime debtor of her "aspirational assimilationist desire" for the "(white settler) American dream" of homeownership and the citizenship and belonging granted through property rights (2012, 497). This dream embodies progress and modernity. For a country like Mexico where modernity can be at times more aspirational than concrete reality, this dream serves as a powerful engine of assimilation for a marginalized citizenry. In Cancún, this settler dream is encapsulated by social housing and is physically constructed over expropriated *ejido* lands.

The foreclosure crisis in Mexico narrates a story of subprime lending and suburbia run amok.[10] In the United States, the subprime debtor is portrayed as either an "illiterate victim" or an "amoral cheat" of the system (See 2012, 495; Stout 2019). These tropes are also associated with depictions of the subprime debtor in the Global South who is marked as working-class, poorly educated, and mestizo.[11] INFONAVIT's representative, portrayed clients who abandoned their houses or participated in debt refusal as a highly mobile workforce. "The residents aren't fixed. . . . The majority come to work seasonally and then they return to their natal communities. It complicates things for us because while in this moment [Cancún] meets their daily needs, but due to their mobility and problems with their pocketbook . . . they abandon their house or stop making payments."[12] The subtext to this critique is that these debtors are transient and irresponsible, and pose a great risk. This representative characterized another debtor as the unwise investor who purchases a "vacation house or beach house. When they encounter economic difficulties, well it becomes easy to get rid of the house, since it's not a home. They stop paying." Once again, the debtor is portrayed as someone who comes from elsewhere and thinks nothing of abandoning this investment (fig. 6). In both cases, the state ends up absorbing the debts of an irresponsible, fugitive population—the mestizo settler run amok. These narratives, however, gloss over the intimate collusion between capital and state to sell the dream of homeownership to working-class Mexicans without taking into account the proximity to commercial centers and jobs, shoddy construction, and crime rates. While the 2008 US housing collapse has been explained in terms of racial subjugation,[13] Mexico's foreclosure crisis has been framed through a class analysis.[14] Its racial dimensions have been overlooked. Keeanga-Yamahtta Taylor (2019) shows that US programs encouraging homeownership among African American families in the 1960s and 1970s led to mass foreclosures. She calls this practice "predatory inclusion" because banks and real estate companies profited from these incentives (2019, 8). In her social history of credit in the United States, Brett Williams (2004) details how the credit industry targets poor communities of color because they are more vulnerable and have less resources to protect themselves against predatory lending. Similar tactics are at work in Mexico, but

FIGURE 6. Abandoned housing for sale. Photograph by author.

the racial dimensions of predatory lending are obscured by the focus on economic inequality. The story of Indigenous peoples as homeowners and as targets of subprime lending has been ignored altogether. Just as foreclosure in colonial America excised Indigenous peoples from foundational fictions, a similar process is taking place in Mexico's foreclosure crisis.

Foreclosure as Discipline

As the financialization of life in Mexico necessitates new systems of regulation, foreclosure proceedings become a disciplinary tactic. Tayyab Mahmud reminds us that "in the neoliberal era the hidden hand of the market and the iron fist of the law worked in concert to forge governmentalities that suture debt with discipline" (2012, 470). Foreclosure becomes a disciplinary practice on behalf of capital and state power to contain, regulate, and punish unruly populations. The relationship established between Mexico's housing funds (INFONAVIT and FOVISSSTE) and private nonbanks like

Tertius reflects these tactics. In many cases, Mexican households undergoing foreclosure cofinanced their mortgage with a UDI loan from a private non-bank like Hipotecaria Su Casita and a loan from a government institution like INFONAVIT or FOVISSSTE. In 2015, approximately five thousand cofinanced loans existed in the state of Quintana Roo.[15] Like Francisco, these clients may have defaulted on their private loan but remained current on their government loan. Representatives of INFONAVIT informed me that the agency does not intervene or mediate foreclosure proceedings in those situations, even when INFONAVIT owns a bigger percentage of the mortgage than the nonbank.[16] Instead, they have ceded control to private companies like Tertius, even if this means their clients will lose their homes and ruin their credit. INFONAVIT and FOVISSSTE will recoup their loss when foreclosed homes are auctioned off. This hands-off approach is rooted in neoliberalism's mantra of personal responsibility that blames the victim for indebtedness.[17] The state is absolved of responsibility and is unwilling to intervene on behalf of its clients, even for clients who are current with their loans.

Under these circumstances, companies like Tertius serve as the extensions—the "arms"—of state power. Tertius is located in a small, nondescript strip mall off of the Avenida Bonampak in Cancún. Before meeting with a loan officer, clients were asked to wait in the spare waiting area, which included a front desk with a receptionist and a few straight-backed chairs for clients and visitors. Clients with appointments were the only ones granted access to the loan officers sitting in desks behind the darkly frosted glass door. Tertius's office in Cancún handles one of the company's largest client portfolios. Nonetheless, few residents of Paseos Kabah were familiar with Tertius's location, nor did they feel empowered to visit this office. This disengagement speaks to the ways the consumer-citizen has been deracialized. While Indigenous migrants actively engaged with political parties and government institutions that provided social services for the poor, they did not have access to or were not familiar with consumer protection agencies like CONDUSEF and PROFECO. These government agencies focus on a deracialized Mexican consumer and expect consumers to seek them out. They have made very little effort to target and interact with Indigenous consumers.[18] In a city like Cancún, where a third of the population is Indigenous, this oversight is troubling, acknowledged Lic. Juan Bosco García Galán, the state delegate of CONDUSEF in 2015. This insight did not prompt CONDUSEF to engage in outreach toward Indigenous people.

As a result, Indigenous migrants rarely sought help from these consumer protection agencies, even when they were looking for ways to safeguard themselves from companies like Tertius.

Tertius adopted a similar approach with its clients. Any face-to-face interaction was the responsibility of the client, not the company. All initial encounters with Tertius were mediated by mail. This lack of face-to-face interaction cultivated an impersonal, transactionary relationship between the corporation and its clients and made it difficult for clients like Francisco to consider visiting the Tertius office to plead their case. A representative of Tertius acknowledged that this approach bred a lack of trust: "The lack of trust by the people is the principal problem [of collecting on defaulted loans]. After paying their mortgage for many years, it was difficult for them to come here to pay. Many people refused to pay because they didn't believe we held their loan, that it was a case of fraud. Everyone was sent a letter. . . . Some came to meet [with us]."[19]

Mariela and Francisco believed that Tertius was driven by profit and was not interested in developing a relationship with its clients, especially since their interactions with company representatives were hostile. Tertius sent two types of representatives into the "field" to negotiate with clients. Loan agents employed by Tertius, called "executives," canvassed social housing. "They visit people," the Tertius representative explained, "they leave a letter, but actually they can negotiate with them. They provide all the information to negotiate." Given the size of Tertius's portfolio, they face a shortage of agents in the field. To fill this gap, Tertius outsources its collection process to three collection agencies. When clients fail to submit payments or respond to Tertius's written requests, "[subcontracted] agencies have the power to negotiate with clients," explained the Tertius representative. However, "these agencies cannot collect money." Nonetheless, these collection agencies relied on punitive measures to collect payments. Subcontractors hired agents who acted as "enforcers" to pressure homeowners to vacate the premises.[20] Francisco recalled, "[they] pressured you, threatened you by telling you that the police were on their way." In some cases, collection agencies demanded payment from clients to cover their own costs. One migrant woman was pressured to pay a five-thousand-peso collection fee. Tertius claimed to be unaware that these subcontractors were using threats of force to make people compliant.[21] Through these strong-arm tactics, working-class residents of Paseos Kabah were disciplined into malleable consumers and citizens and habituated to become less reliant on support from the state.

The high vacancy rates in Cancún have forced INFONAVIT to take on more debt than this agency is comfortable holding. A representative explained that this debt has prompted the federal government to warn them: "There is this phenomenon. Be careful, do not provide credit."[22] Being held accountable by its central agency in Mexico City has compelled the Cancún branch of INFONAVIT to enforce stricter measures for doling out loans. The representative stated that it's not a policy. "Simply put, we're restricting credit disbursements to address this phenomenon." This retrenchment signals to the public that the state is not in their corner and ends up punishing the residents of Cancún instead of the subprime lenders who created the problem.

Foreclosure also disciplines by blaming victims (See 2012; Stout 2019). Tertius accused homeowners undergoing foreclosure of being swindlers. The Tertius representative explained that they worked with two types of clients, distrustful clients and cheats. "There are people," she proclaimed, "who will say anything to not pay. Some people claimed that they hadn't been granted permission to transfer their debt, even when [this permission] was written into the contract."[23] Tertius was less willing to negotiate with the latter type of clients because it was easier to recover their funds once the house entered auction proceedings. According to Tertius's representative, Su Casita was partially responsible for attracting these types of clients with their philosophy of "If he/she breathes, they are clients." As a result, "everyone was given a loan. Even people who could not prove their income. . . . It was typical of the zone or the region. Their income is not fixed. They are reliant on an informal economy." By blaming the victim, the state and corporations shed their responsibility to help homeowners, even as the state spent millions to bail out bankrupt companies.

Yet the reality of why homeowners defaulted on their loans is complex. Mariela and Francisco made numerous attempts to renegotiate the terms of their loan. With the aid of a lawyer, Francisco's sister was able to negotiate a new *convenio* or contract with Su Casita before it was purchased by Tertius that reduced her monthly mortgage payment from 900 pesos to 600 pesos for the next five years. Feeling optimistic, Mariela and Francisco planned to contact this lawyer, but she "disappeared" before they could do so. The contract turned out to be unenforceable. "[Francisco's sister] recently received a notice informing her that she had to make her house payments because it now belonged to Tertius," explained Mariela. "Yet Su Casita continues to demand payments from her. . . . Tertius is collecting everything, even the *convenios* with Su Casita. They don't care if you are still paying Su Casita. [Tertius informed them:] 'If you are paying Su Casita, go ahead and donate your money. But with us, it's a new contract.'" This confusion made it difficult to determine whom to pay and whom to trust. The new mortgage payment plans provided by Tertius were demoralizing because the payments were too high, making it impossible for families to make ends meet. Francisco's payment to INFONAVIT was Mex$540 monthly. Tertius's contract asked for payment of Mex$2300 monthly. "It's a lot of money [to make both payments]," exclaimed Francisco. "I earn a minimum wage salary. From where [will I come up with the money]? What are we going to do? We don't know who to pay. I made the decision to not pay anyone." Defaulting on a loan was the outcome of a complex calculus based on income, rumor, and past and present experiences with company agents.

This strategy placed Mariela and Francisco at great risk. They quickly learned to keep their door barred against the debt collection agents who were dispatched to remove them from their home. Mariela bore the brunt of their threats because she worked from home, unlike Francisco who worked six days a week, sometimes double shifts. She was in charge of dealing with all the paperwork and with dispatching the agents who knocked on her door and demanded payment. Even though Francisco's name was on the loan, it was Mariela's job to stave off eviction. To do so, she quit her job as a domestic servant and set up a small grocery store in the first floor of her house. Self-employment give her the flexibility to meet with lawyers, photocopy documents, and organize neighbors. These tasks were onerous but manageable. What Mariela found difficult and what eroded her spirit was dealing with threats of violence by agents who worked in collusion with local police. At times, these threats made her afraid to leave her house, making her feel like a prisoner in her home.

Mariela's experience was compounded by the fact that Indigenous women are at great risk for gender and state violence (Goeman 2017; Speed 2019). Mariela is petite and very soft-spoken. Her facial features, accent, and speech patterns—her Spanish is inflected with a distinctive Yucatecan accent and borrows from Yucatec Maya linguistic structures—mark her as Indigenous in a city largely dominated by a mestizo population and where discrimination and violence against Indigenous people is commonplace. I have personally witnessed the pejorative treatment Maya people experience in Cancún. Maya women are especially vulnerable to violence and face harassment on the street by employers, government administrators, and the police. My collaborators have shared stories of these devastating encounters with me but asked me not disclose these details, because they do not wish to broadcast these shameful and traumatic encounters. The point I make here is that this violence is real and occurs on a frequent basis. For Mariela, having debt collectors and the police knock on her door triggered these traumatic experiences.

As Clara Han (2012) poignantly attests, the consumer-based individualism of neoliberal reforms has deleterious and corrosive effects on the mental health of urban residents. In Mariela and Francisco's case, the waiting also produced a general sense of anxiety that never went away and was reflected in the tension that seeped into their bodies whenever they talked about foreclosure proceedings. This stress was not good for Francisco, who was diabetic. He found it difficult to regulate his blood sugar, forcing him to miss work periodically. Mariela gained weight because she was stuck inside all day. Losing a home forecloses possibilities. This narrowing of a life, as Noelle Stout (2019) evocatively demonstrates for families who lost their homes in California, erodes a sense of self and hollows out dreams. This frustration could have easily turned Mariela and Francisco against each other, but they told me they felt "more united" and determined to wait it out.

Francisco and Mariela purchased the bulk of their home with a loan from INFONAVIT, to which they continue to make timely payments. However, by refusing to intervene, INFONAVIT ceded its right to the private mortgage company and facilitated this company's efforts to dispossess Mariela and Francisco. In Kuchmil, Mariela and Francisco could make claims on the state to come to their aid using the language of patrimony and Indigenous rights. In Cancún, ejido lands have been privatized, and Indigenous rights hold little sway in local politics. Mariela and Francisco are encouraged by the state and capital to view the customs and social relations that guide ejido land tenure practices as outmoded frames of reference. In its stead, the house, with its emphasis on the nuclear family, individual debt, and personal responsibility—has become symbolic of the types of relationships they should form with the government, with their neighbors, and with each other. It is telling that Sebastián Fernández Cortina, who served as Director of INFONAVIT for fifteen years, emphatically stated, "INFONAVIT is not a central housing agency. . . . We are a finance agency."[24] This may appear to be a contradictory statement, but it reflects the values underpinning social housing, where individualized debt becomes the principal nexus for social relations. Georgia Hartman (forthcoming) suggests that transforming the home from a social good into a financial commodity is undermining working-class Mexican's notions of homes as patrimonial possessions. For Mariela and Francisco, the discipline that is central to this transition has prompted them to see their modern home as a new form of *esclavitud* and to critique the mortgage lending business as "fraud," in collusion with the state. The Mexican government is once again perceived as a police state in service of global capital.

On Waiting

Based on his ethnographic study of people seeking state services in Argentina, Javier Auyero contends that "[d]omination works . . . through yielding to the powers of others; and it is experienced as a waiting time: waiting hopefully and then frustratingly for others to make decisions, and in effect surrendering to the authority of others" (2012, 4). Similarly, as they wait for Tertius to foreclose on their house, Mariela and Francisco learn subordination. Yet Mariela and Francisco also cultivate insubordination against Tertius and the state when they convert waiting into a process of "waiting out." Estimating that they had a decade before the courts foreclosed on their home, Mariela and Francisco used this time to come up with multiple strategies for keeping their home. Almost a decade later, they remained in their house. To wait out the state and capital also becomes a mode of living where inhabiting one's home and participating in community gatherings become collective acts of resistance.

To avoid undermining or placing at risk negotiations with Tertius, I will not share Mariela and Francisco's current playbook for circumventing foreclosure. As Linda Tuhiwai Smith (2012) reminds us, decolonizing methodologies entail practices and ethics that recognize Indigenous people as agents, not objects of study, and call upon us to be cognizant of the way research can be appropriated to the detriment of Indigenous people. Safeguarding the trust Mariela and Francisco have granted me as their collaborator and friend also animates this decision. Instead, I share dead ends, strategies that delayed but did not stave off foreclosure and thus were eventually abandoned.

Collective organizing was the first strategy deployed by the households in Paseos Kabah. Based on their experience with the ejido, Francisco and Mariela understood the power of the collective to make demands on government and to shape a political future. In contrast, lone individuals hold very little sway in government or politics, and especially not against corporations. "It benefits [Tertius and the government] if we aren't organized," observed Francisco. The residents of Paseos Kabah were approached by several grassroots organizations that specialized in organizing urban neighborhoods. Like their neighbors, Mariela and Francisco rejected these offers because these organizations demanded costly monthly membership fees. They heard rumors that these organizations were "opportunists" who were "untrustworthy" because it wasn't clear what services the membership fees paid for. They were also wary of lawyers who claimed they could help, but "didn't know anything about property rights."

A friend introduced Francisco to a lawyer who had experience with land rights in Cancún. After being unable to renegotiate their mortgages individually, a cluster of households on Mariela and Francisco's block hired this lawyer to represent them collectively. Since Francisco understood that "we needed to be organized to protect ourselves against eviction," he rallied forty families to meet with the lawyer with the intent of establishing a collective. However, only five families were willing to join the collective; the others were unable to see eye to eye. Francisco explained, "There are different cultures, so we couldn't come to an agreement." The residents of Paseos Kabah come from diverse states in Mexico, including Yucatán, Tabasco, and Veracruz, among others, and found it difficult to trust people with divergent backgrounds and customs. The law office charged each household in the collective an initial fee of one thousand pesos. Any additional fees incurred for legal filings would be itemized, which made it possible for families to keep track of costs and opt for alternative routes when they did not have available funds. The law firm spent one year fruitlessly trying to renegotiate the mortgages. By January 2015, Mariela and Francisco had paid Mex$22,000 "to fight without any guarantee" of winning their case. This collective effort was disbanded as each family sought alternative routes by which to keep their homes.

Mariela and Francisco were disheartened by this outcome, but they were not deterred. Their efforts to organize a collective front against eviction may have failed to come to fruition, but this failure did not translate into the demise of audible forms of protest. The urban dispossessed, Bayat reminds us, are made up of "social *nonmovements* of fragmented and inaudible collectives . . . [that] quietly imping[e] on the propertied and powerful, and on society at large" through everyday practices like squatting and street vending (2010, 17). After the collapse of the collective, Mariela and Francisco turned to friends for recommendations for lawyers who were nimble at manipulating the law. They refused to give up. "We are fighting. . . . The worst outcome would be for me to lose the house without a fight," explained Francisco. They considered themselves in good company since most of their neighbors were in the same predicament. Cancún has a vacancy rate of 10 percent, but housing developments like Paseos Kabah have a foreclosure rate closer to the national rate of 14.2 percent, which is double the vacancy rate in the United States.[25] It's important to note that vacancy rates in Mexico are not solely attributable to foreclosures. As INFONAVIT loans became more readily accessible, individuals used this loan to purchase a second home as an investment strategy (Monkkonen 2014). It is these homes, when abandoned, that augment the vacancy rate. But Paavo Monkkonen (2018) also points out that cities with high rates of government mortgage lending experience higher vacancy rates.

Mariela and Francisco's reliance on legal strategies to combat foreclosure resembles strategies used by social activists throughout Latin America to protest neoliberal policies and social injustice. These organizing tools—the foot dragging, collective protests, and lawsuits—circulate widely amid social activists in Cancún and beyond. What inspired these calls to action is what is distinctive about this couple's circumstances. When Francisco explained that most of the neighbors facing foreclosure vacated their home within a few years, I asked him why not decamp and begin anew? They could funnel the thousands of pesos needed to settle this dispute into a plot of land. (The dispute prevented Francisco from soliciting another loan from INFONAVIT, limiting his future housing options.) Mariela and Francisco drew from a history of robust collective resistance by Maya communities in southeastern Yucatán. Their ancestors were devotees of the *Santa Cruz* and successfully launched a revolt against the Mexican government that lasted fifty years; for some Maya communities, this revolt is ongoing. Mariela and Francisco are members of an ejido community that taught them to fight injustice by using every means possible. "[We learned] from our parents' initiative," explained Francisco. "They are fighters who refuse to be abused. They refuse it. They fight." Mariela and Francisco were involved in their community's long-standing battle to defend their autonomy by securing an ejido land title and by protecting communal rights to land (Castellanos 2010b). This campaign, under the guidance of Francisco's father, relied heavily on the law as a weapon of resistance. "[Our parents] fight with the legal means at their disposal," Francisco confirmed. By identifying their parents and their community as the inspiration for their debt refusal, Mariela and Francisco draw parallels between their struggle for homeownership and previous and ongoing struggles for Maya autonomy. The frame of reference that inspired the couple's will to resist is grounded in place and memory and in a temporality where the past is never past, but ongoing.[26] Leanne Betasamosake Simpson (2017) asserts that "the kinds of alternatives [Indigenous people] are compelled to embody are profoundly systemic . . . based on a deep reciprocity" and rooted in place. Forging an alternative present, she expands, entails engaging with "Indigenous life as it has always unfolded." By associating resistance with debt refusal, Francisco also situates his legal battle against foreclosure within the *longue durée* of an Indigenous politics of refusal that strives against colonial and settler colonial strictures and structures. Audra Simpson (2014) argues that ethnographic portraits of Indigenous life served to justify the administration and dispossession of Indigenous peoples, while failing to capture Indigenous refusals that fell outside these homogeneous narratives. Francisco's refusal decenters narratives that conflate Indians with land and rural spaces by riveting our attention on Indigenous urban homeownership in the wake of the global housing collapse.

In light of this history, Mariela and Francisco considered legal frameworks a tactic rather than an impediment. They were aware that foreclosures and evictions take time. Francisco clarified that the legal battle "prolonged the time they needed to procure more money" to stave off eviction. By taking advantage of this delay, they were able to remain in their home while they waited out Tertius and the state. More important, the lag gave them time to find another lawyer to take on their case. Their new lawyer was more proactive in using countersuits to delay foreclosure and to pressure Tertius to negotiate. Although they requested that I not share these legal strategies, they did wish to emphasize that they were fighting the law with the law. "We will prevail. . . . It's legal because [the strategies] are based on the law. We're relying on legal precedent that challenges the government. Because the laws of the government are set up to make us pay." This process comes at a steep cost. Mariela and Francisco have already spent approximately Mex$60,000 (close to US$3,000 in today's dollars).

For Tertius, time is its own predicament. Tertius may have purchased these loans for cents on the dollar, but their objective is to recuperate as much money as possible. On the one hand, convincing a client to catch up on payments allows the company to move this case off its docket and receive a payment in full of a debt pegged to an escalating dollar. This process requires that its agents spend time with clients who are justifiably skittish about the corporate takeover. These overtures are friendly at first but can quickly become combative. On the other hand, a speedy resolution to foreclosure proceedings makes it possible to sell the house at auction, providing Tertius with a reduction in caseload, a quick windfall from the profit of selling the house at market rate, and fosters goodwill with INFONAVIT because it takes this loan off its docket. With the aid of the state, waiting becomes a means through which Tertius instructs its clients to follow neoliberal capital's dictum of accumulation by dispossession.

Francisco lamented, "What the mortgage lender is doing is unjust." In light of this injustice, his and Mariela's refusal to let go of the dream of homeownership reflects what Sarita See perceives to be an effort "to find better ways to cohabit and live with one another, unowning rather than disowning one another in a world dedicated to a radically different kind of dispossession" (2012, 511). Because judicial proceedings are not swift and allow room for negotiation, Francisco and Mariela can wait out the system by drawing on patterns of resistance and refusal that are grounded in Indigenous traditions of collective land tenure and in struggles for autonomy.

Reimagining Citizenship

Recent critiques highlight the social isolation and segregation that plague Mexico's social housing (Monkkonen 2012; Reyes Ruiz del Cueto 2013). I encountered this sense of isolation and political cynicism when I, along with two survey assistants (Adriana González Neri and Kristina Silva Ara) from the Universidad del Caribe, conducted a housing survey of one hundred households in Paseos Kabah. We interviewed every third household, but the high vacancy rate forced us to skip to the fourth, even fifth or sixth house. When we knocked on doors, residents peered out questioningly from their windows before hesitantly answering their doors to strangers. Most times our conversations took place through a tiny crack in the door or while residents stood behind the safety of their metal screen door. Occasionally we were invited inside. The friendliest residents were those who hailed from the state of Yucatán. When they heard me speak Spanish with a Yucatecan accent, they welcomed us into their home. Linguistic differences reflected the cultural divides that exist in a city of migrants. Francisco and Mariela found it easier to trust a neighbor from their home state of Yucatán than one from Guerrero due to shared cultural and linguistic practices.

These cultural differences were exacerbated by political cleavages. During the survey collection, the first question we were asked was the name of the political party we represented. At first, we were puzzled by this query until it was pointed out that it was an election year and we were wearing white T-shirts and blue pants, the colors of the National Action Party (Partido Acción Nacional or PAN). Based on her experiences canvassing for UCI, Nereida, explained that in the past neighbors were willing to talk to you, to sign petitions, but now "no one will share [that information]. They've seen that it's a business." Since political organizations are known for rewarding people who collect signatures, people are hesitant to participate unless it directly benefits them. Residents were also wary of political organizations making promises that remain unfulfilled. A few families had asked local politicians for help fighting their foreclosure, without results. We were also turned away by many residents who did not believe we were who we claimed to be. To confirm their identities, Adriana and Kristina carried their university IDs while conducting the survey. This standoffish behavior served as a protective measure against government and political machinations.

Francisco's efforts to create a neighborhood association against foreclosure were hindered by the lack of trust among his neighbors. While atomization and isolation can impede collaboration, they do not fully abrogate collective organizing. *Colonias* and urban centers in Latin America are spaces rife for reimagining citizenship (Holston 2008; Murphy 2015). Francisco established a neighborhood block association to monitor the arrival of debt collection agents intent on evicting families. Although Francisco was not successful in organizing a mass movement against foreclosure, he did manage to bring together a few families on his block; they pooled their financial resources to hire a lawyer to educate them on housing law and their rights as homeowners and squatters. They also met with grassroots organizations in other neighborhoods to learn about strategies for resisting foreclosure. Through these practices, Mariela and Francisco developed strong ties with their neighbors and collected tactics against foreclosure from their neighbors and friends, which they applied to individual cases. Foreclosure proceedings form part of a system that individualizes debt. By sharing individual foreclosure strategies, migrants convert these tactics into a collective practice that refutes efforts to construct a nation of debtors. In response to threats of foreclosure, residents of Paseos Kabah have carved out new spaces for social solidarity and social change.

Under these circumstances, atomization, abandonment, and resistance become the means through which the residents of Paseos Kabah survive in Cancún's periphery. These defensive measures form part of what Asef Bayat calls the "quiet encroachment of the ordinary." "A key attribute of quiet encroachments," Bayat explains, "is that while advances are made quietly, individually, and gradually, the defense of their gains is often, although not always, collective and audible" (2010, 48). For Indigenous communities, public manifestations of collective resistance, like the Zapatista rebellion, are audible forms by which to challenge neoliberal policies of development. But these practices are not always possible, especially when neoliberal financial structures impose atomization through the individualization of debt. In her study of social movements in Cancún, Christine Kray found that "power was too diffuse and all-encompassing to be resisted" (2016, 68). She explains that "social movements are stalled because what people can resist (the state) offers no clear front and what they want to resist (global inequalities) seems impossible" (85). By waiting out the state, Francisco and Mariela transform quiet encroachment and bureaucratization into audible forms of resistance to Indigenous dispossession.

Social housing in Mexico has expropriated ejido land into miniaturized versions of the settler dream of homeownership. Mortgage debt binds migrants to Cancún's shifting economic future and underscores generational shifts in the urbanization and monetization of land, labor, and debt. Maya migrants entering the housing market for the first time experience new forms of subjectivity that require them to cleave away from land tenure practices rooted in the ejido to imagine new ways of relating to home and community. As they have witnessed their neighbors' evictions, Mariela and Francisco know they can't stave off eviction with grassroots community tactics of resistance. Instead, they are constructing an alternative approach that regrounds their ties to home and land based on rural traditions and inspired by Indigenous struggles for autonomy.

5

Eviction
Invoking Indigenous Resistance

IN 2012 IN CANCÚN, twenty-two families residing in the shantytown of Colonia Mario Villanueva sued the landowner for fraud. These families sought to legitimize their land claims so they could begin building more permanent housing structures. Doing so would transform them from squatters to homeowners, granting them legal rights to their home. Two years later, a judge ruled in favor of the landowner and granted permission to evict these families. *Colonos* (*colonia* residents or settlers) rallied to prevent this expulsion. Magda, a Maya migrant living in the colonia and one of the leaders of the protest, encouraged the claimants to seek help from Antorcha Campesina, a grassroots organization with a long history of defending *campesino* (peasant) rights that had recently begun organizing urban residents. Magda's family had worked with Antorcha when the organization helped her hometown maintain their *ejido* (communal landholding) rights. Why did *colonos* turn to Antorcha, an organization with limited experience in urban settings, instead of established urban organizations like Only Settlers' Front (FUC)? While the residents of the colonia come from different states in Mexico, the women leading the charge were from rural Maya towns. Instead of modeling the campaign to regularize land titles after urban social movements, these women turned toward Indigenous rural land struggles as models for social justice. By invoking the concept of the commons in an urban setting where private property is entangled with diminishing state support for communal land tenure and public services, Indigenous leaders like Magda frame their struggle for housing as rooted in communal Indigenous land tenure practices and as a form of resistance to the state and global capital.

I was first exposed to the plight of Colonia Mario Villanueva when Magda, whom I've known since she was a child, invited me to her home in December of 2014. Magda thought I might be interested in their legal battle because I was studying Indigenous homeownership. As I documented their struggle, I interviewed families in the colonia and the leaders of Antorcha Campesina. I also observed meetings colonia residents held with government officials and participated in the Antorcha campaign, including leafleting neighborhoods and attending political rallies and community meetings. I spent most of my time with Maya women like Magda who served as the community liaisons with Antorcha and as the political leaders of their colonia.

The Making of a Colonia

When migrants arrived in mass to build the tourist center of Cancún beginning in the 1970s, they were housed in camps in improvised tents and communal barracks or established informal settlements in the jungle and ejidos located north of the city (McLean n.d.). These camps and settlements were rudimentary, lacking basic sewer service and running water. By the mid-1970s, in response to increasing land invasions to accommodate new arrivals, the city, in coordination with state and federal agencies, began the process of regularizing colonias by helping residents acquire land titles and by expediting the installation of public services. Thus began a process of periodic land regularizations that was severely hampered by the municipality's limited public works budget (ibid.). Not surprisingly, mobilizing to access affordable housing and public services became a means by which to organize the working class and consolidate political power among local party bosses (Kray 2006, also see Herrera 2017).

Today almost all the land within Cancún's urban zone has been regulated. The majority of Cancún's unregulated settlements (sixty-eight in total in 2015) are located along or right outside the edge of the urban periphery.[1] Colonia Mario Villanueva is an exception because it is located within Cancún's urban zone. The push toward the eradication and regularization of so-called "slums" and "shantytowns" is happening globally (Neuwirth 2006). This trend is a historical outgrowth of a process that James Scott refers to as the "last great enclosure movement" intended to monetize land (2010, 4). This monetization is rooted in neoliberal policies predicated on what David Harvey calls "accumulation by dispossession," where common lands are privatized for the benefit of capital and the state, instead of labor (2004, 74). In Cancún, these enclosures become "'nested' instruments of flexible privatization" to benefit neoliberal capital, to the detriment of working-class neighborhoods and colonias (Córdoba Azcárate, Baptista, and Domínguez Rubio 2014). In the case of Colonia Mario Villanueva, where land prices have escalated as the city has expanded, this monetization benefits the private landowner.

Although now considered to be private property, Colonia Mario Villanueva was formerly part of an ejido. With the establishment of the tourist center, *ejidatarios* were tempted to informally sell or rent tracts of land. After agrarian reform permitted the privatization and legal sale of ejido land, many *ejidatarios* elected to divide up ejidos and began renting or selling off small tracts of land to individuals. But these transactions, along with land redistributed from the government's land reserves (much of which was expropriated ejido land), could not accommodate the overwhelming number of migrants looking for housing, prompting land invasions coordinated by organizations like FUC (McLean n.d.). In light of Cancún's early history of land invasions, the current landowner of Colonia Mario Villanueva most likely procured this tract through squatting. The colonia's location on the outskirts of Cancún's periphery, next to Región 225, made it difficult for the landowner to carve up the property into lots for sale. Few people wanted to live so far from downtown, the transportation hub of the Riviera Maya. By car, the colonia's proximity to downtown and the hotel zone was manageable (approximately 6 miles and 12 miles, respectively), but by bus it was remote, requiring multiple stops, and took close to one hour of travel each way. In 2004, however, with the support of INFONAVIT, large tracts of social housing were built next to the colonia. Improved roads, new and more direct bus and taxi routes, and modest prices made this housing accessible and attractive despite the distance from downtown. The landowner saw this as an opportunity to make a profit. She divided a portion of her property into one hundred individual parcels of land, pricing each lot at Mex$68,000. Her husband advertised the sale with handwritten notices on cardboard stock that he tacked to electricity posts of the new *fraccionamiento* Villas Otoch. A parcel of land was secured with a deposit (Mex$1,000–12,500 at the owner's discretion), followed by monthly payments over a five-year period. These plots did not include basic services like paved roads, legal electricity, or potable water. Landowners of informal settlements in Cancún rarely incorporate public services prior to selling lots on the private market. Building public service infrastructure is considered the state's responsibility once informal settlements are regulated and incorporated within municipal boundaries. The parcels were quickly sold to migrants who couldn't afford or wished to avoid tract housing. These sales were informal transactions. All payments were made in the name of the landowner's husband, who publicly claimed ownership. Receipts for payments consisted of a typed sheet of paper stating the amount paid, date, and signature of the landowner's husband. The landowner did not sign these documents but, according to *colonos*, she was present at some of these transactions.

The distinction between public and private property on land previously or currently held in common can be ambiguous and can operate on multiple scales (Nonini 2006). Once squatters occupy ejido land, this land can be simultaneously classified as communal land and private property. The blurring of legal categorizations forms part of the history of informal settlements. As Brodwyn Fischer notes, the majority of informal settlements in Latin America "originate in roughly similar patterns of invasion, negotiations, and petty profiteering" (2014, 2). Ownership can also become a fuzzy concept in colonias where *invasores* (squatters) claim rights to land. The language of invasion is a discursive strategy historically deployed by migrants and politicians to make claims on the state (McLean n.d.). Politicians and local newspapers describe Colonia Mario Villanueva as a squatter settlement, even though the residents claim they are not *invasores* who settled without permission from the landowner. This discourse renders *colonos'* claims suspect and unenforceable. It also marks colonias as spaces of danger. When I asked a representative of the nonprofit Fundación Hogares if their programs in Villas Otoch would be available to colonia residents, I was warned to avoid the colonia because these *"invasores"* were responsible for the crime perpetrated in neighboring *fraccionamientos*. This representative lived in Mexico City but had flown out to meet with the staff in the Cancún office. He wielded this stereotype without providing any proof to back it up. This discursive terrain of illegality and criminality hinders the colonia's efforts to transform informal property relations into state-sanctioned rights.

Due to the informal nature of their land claims, *colonos* initially did not expect the landowner to provide public services. The colonia has no electricity, running water, roads, or sanitation system. In Cancún, this type of infrastructural development falls under the purview of the state, but the state will not provide these services to informal settlements until they are legally incorporated into the city's urban plan. Each homeowner must determine how to access these services, be it by borrowing power from a neighbor, creating a shared well, or installing their own generator. With the expansion of social housing, the land surrounding the colonia was developed into tract housing, bringing a host of public services, from new roads to electrical grids. As a result, the colonia has become centrally located to shopping malls, grocery stores, schools, and express bus routes.

In spite of this urban growth, the colonia remains a shantytown with homes built out of cardboard, plywood, and recycled materials. Electrical wires zigzagging from house to house are strewn on the ground connecting water pumps and hang in the air protruding from homemade adapters tapping the city's electrical posts (fig. 7). The roads, though widened to give access to cars and trucks, remain unpaved and pitted with sharp limestone rocks. The majority of the one hundred families that live here refuse to invest in building concrete block homes before the settlement is urbanized and land titles authorized. The process of urbanization can alter lot boundaries depending on where roads are mapped out, and spending thousands of pesos to construct a house that they may not be able to keep is too steep a risk. Until then, the colonia remains temporary, caught between a legacy of ejido politics and haphazard urban development.

FIGURE 7. Tapping into the electrical grid. Photograph by Seung Kyum Kim. Reprinted with permission.

Land Politics

Colonos became tired of waiting for regularization. A few families in Colonia Mario Villanueva sold the rights to their plot in order to make back the money they spent on building materials and improvements. Rights to plots were typically resold for prices ranging from 2,000 to 5,000 pesos. This was the route by which Magda and her husband Iván settled in the colonia. Their participation in the legal battle is representative of *colonos'* experiences. I met Magda when she was a child living in Kuchmil. She was originally from Sab'ak (a pseudonym), a rural Maya pueblo and ejido in Yucatán, but as a child she temporarily resided with her aunt while she attended school in Kuchmil. She became my guide to the colonia. In 2009, Magda and Iván purchased the right to a plot with a small one-room house on site for 5,000 pesos from a family who decided to sell out. In addition, Magda and Iván negotiated a contract with the husband of the landowner (who they believed *was* the landowner) where they agreed to pay a deposit of 10,000 pesos in monthly installments of 1,000 pesos.

Given this contract, Iván and Magda did not consider themselves to be squatters. In the popular imaginary, squatting connotes illegality and pathology. As Brodwyn Fischer points out, "the settlements' photogenic misery allows them to serve as potent symbols in polemical global debates about poverty, capitalism, race, and state failure. The instant identification of these settlements with the 'subaltern' makes them the natural locale for radical critiques of the powers that be. . . . Portraits of the informal cities that focus only on their pathologies, or their transformative potential, can easily miss their constitutive role in extant urban cultural and power relations, the settlements' functional vitality in the here and now" (2014, 2). Magda and Iván overlooked this poverty because they were attracted by the strong sense of family and community shared by *colonos*, which reminded them of their Indigenous pueblos. Colonia life is organized around community consensus, with social relations solidified through fictive and biological kin networks. Iván and Magda were encouraged to move to the colonia by Iván's cousin who already lived there. *Colonos* share resources, including building materials, babysitting, backyards, and access to wells. With its abundant foliage and open patio space, the colonia has the feel of a rural village. Community meetings are held to make collective decisions regarding demands for government resources, disputes with the landowner, and participation in Antorcha Campesina.

Maya migrants like Magda and Iván consider life in the colonia to be deeply connected to the history of the ejido. Article 27 of the 1917

Mexican constitution provided the legal foundation for ejido communities by making land inalienable, guaranteeing usufruct rights to agrarian communities that held communal status, and mandating land redistribution. Mexico's 1992 constitutional reforms recognize Indigenous peoples' right to self-determination, but how this is expressed varies at the local, state, and federal levels (Speed 2008). Maya people in Yucatán conceive the right to self-determination as tied to ejido land tenure practices, in which ejido members have the right to work the land and to pass down usufruct rights to their children. Agrarian reform in 1992 made it possible to privatize ejido lands, but Magda and Iván come from ejido communities that have elected to maintain communal ownership. Ejido members are provided with a house plot, access to communal forest lands, and a parcel of agricultural land that is rotated every few years. They are required to participate in mandatory communal work; agricultural and social life is regulated by consensus. Indeed, the ejido forms part of a moral economy that regulates the social behavior of its members (Castellanos 2010b). The general assembly, made up of ejido members and led by the *comisariado ejidal* (the ejido's governing body), resolves land disputes and personal conflicts. Although ejido membership is predominantly male, women participate in the general assembly when issues pertaining to the social welfare of the community arise (Castellanos 2010b). This approach to land tenure reflects a long history of Maya struggles for autonomy from debt peonage and foreign rule in the Yucatán Peninsula (Reed 1964; Sullivan 1989). For many Maya people, land represents autonomy from the state. Yet they are aware that autonomy in neoliberal Mexico is contingent on state support for land rights and agricultural production, and state subsidies for health care, education, and nutrition. Nonetheless, the ideologies of ejido production "travel" and seep into Maya migrants' understanding of life in Cancún (Re Cruz 1996a, 1996b; 2003).

As Maya migrants settle in urban centers that are built on Indigenous lands, the desire for autonomy remains, but it must be adapted to urban markets and government bureaucracy. Magda and Iván acknowledge that the government support provided to Indigenous pueblos is limited in an urban context. "In the pueblos," Magda explains, "the government gives when it can. . . . We want the government to offer us [migrants] the same support, the same programs in health, nutrition, education. . . . The government has the same obligation [to provide] health care, education, housing."[2] Unfortunately, the state perceives its obligations differently in an urban context, where Indigenous rights are not recognized beyond ejido boundaries and where Indigenous migrants constitute a minority with scant political power. In her study of street vendors in Cancún, Lorena Muñoz shows that claiming rights to the city does not always presume adhering to neoliberal terms of engagement, but instead reflects efforts by street vendors to "creat[e] their own socioeconomic opportunities through vending systems outside state-sanctioned disciplining systems" (2018, 14). What Magda proposes, then, clashes with neoliberal models of urban life because it hearkens to a model of reciprocity and social commitment.

A Retreating State

Iván acknowledged that living in a shantytown can be a miserable existence. At first, their one-room house consisted of a dirt floor, lacked electricity and water, and was only accessible by a narrow footpath. It was a "grand challenge" to raise a toddler without basic services. "We may come from a rural village, but we had normal houses. . . . You become accustomed to living in a tourist center and you never imagine that you will live in a place like this. You arrive thinking that you will have a nicer home, a better future." Indeed, when migrants arrive in Cancún, they rent rooms or stay with relatives whose homes include amenities like sewage systems, running water, and electricity. Iván comes from the southeastern Maya town of Peto, a pre-Columbian town in Yucatán that fell under colonial rule in 1549 and was involved in chicle production in the early 1900s. With approximately twenty thousand residents, it now serves as the municipal seat for twenty-one ejido communities and has extended diasporic ties with the United States, maintaining them through its Facebook page. Iván's parents are *ejidatarios*. His house in Peto was modest, with adobe walls and cement floors. Yet compared to his house in Cancún, with its cardboard walls and dirt floors, his home in Peto seems palatial. He explains, "Unfortunately, you arrive in this place [Cancún] and you encounter many things that you never imagined or dreamed of. . . . You arrive and see the polar opposite." For Iván, moving to the shanty was one of the most "difficult moments" because "he wasn't accustomed to this type of life." Although his house is now connected to the electrical grid and has expanded to include a kitchen, bathroom, and bedroom, it still lacks flooring, sturdy walls, and access to running water (fig. 8). Iván laments, as he waves his hand to encompass the shantytown, "how is it possible to live in paradise and allow this to be tolerated?" Living with dignity under these conditions becomes an everyday

FIGURE 8. Housing in Colonia Mario Villanueva. Photograph by Seung Kyum Kim. Reprinted with permission.

struggle and requires an ongoing reimagining of the past, present, and future (Han 2012).

Iván calls attention to the violence endemic to urban poverty, especially in a place professing luxury and adventure for the wealthy and foreign, while the majority of the workforce lacks access to basic services. Without these services, colonias like Mario Villanueva will remain impoverished and marginalized. As communal land tracts have become privatized (Nonini 2006), the state has evaded its responsibility to provide public services to unregulated settlements. Urban studies scholars point out that poverty is a form of structural violence, but Akhil Gupta proposes that in most cases, this violence is an "arbitrary outcome" caused by state indifference and neglect (2012, 24). In Cancún, the failure to enforce environmental regulation and a lack of urban planning for the working poor has produced this dichotomy of misery/paradise; the city and tourist economy are dependent on cheap disposable migrant labor and yet very little is invested toward their reproductive costs (Castellanos 2010a). As Fischer notes, informal neighborhoods are "thoroughly entwined with formal urbanity [because] [t]he formal city profits economically and politically from the slum's illegality" (2014, 1). This development model produces what Matilde Córdoba Azcárate and her colleagues refer to as a "mutual dissociation" of indifference (2014, 66). Moreover, this dissociation stems from settler colonial and colonial structures that underpin the configuration of urban space as exclusionary and disciplinary practices that expose Maya migrants to racialized and gendered violence (e.g., Dorries et al. 2019; Horn 2019; Jackson et al. 2018; Walker et al. 2013).

For colonia residents, the absence of basic services in Colonia Mario Villanueva represents the state's retreat and abandonment, and reflects settler colonial logics that negate humanity and relationality. According to Magda, it is difficult to live a dignified life, "to be human," without basic services of "water, electricity, roads, and housing, which is the most important of all." Migrants argue that it is the state's responsibility to provide these services. "It's necessary that the government provide public services," exclaims Magda. Yet landowners can avoid making concessions by stalling indefinitely until the courts rule in their favor. The state's recent promotion of social housing was intended to address Cancún's housing crisis by providing alternatives to informal settlements. Article 4 in Mexico's constitution advocates for all citizens to have access to a "dignified home" that is soundly constructed with access to basic services. Colonia Mario Villanueva represents a challenge to making this dream possible. For Magda, Indigenous pueblos provide a blueprint for how the state should treat its citizens. "We don't benefit from the privileges held by *pueblitos* [small pueblos]. Here we need the government to intervene to regulate the colonias. In contrast since the *pueblitos* are municipal headquarters, it's easy to meet with the *comisario* [mayor], have him sign your documents, and authorize your land title." In pueblos, the *comisario*, a familiar figurehead who is Indigenous, represents the state. This level of familiarity is absent in Cancún, where the state is represented by mestizo elites who make it difficult to meet face to face and whose interests benefit themselves and global capital, not Indigenous migrants. Migrants are treated as urban citizens, not as Indigenous *pueblos*, a process that deracializes them and transforms a relationship with the state that has been guided by an Indigenous rights framework to one that is now marked by a discourse of urban malaise and pathology. By remaining "at a distance" and refusing to pressure the landowner to reach a settlement, Magda proclaims, "the government has failed us." This sentiment of failure and abandonment also plagues social movements headed by organizations like FUC, resulting in what Kray (2006) characterizes as "stalled social movements."

Even if "[t]he local rootedness of informal cities renders most generalizations about them fanciful, easily belied by one or a thousand divergent experiences," Fischer notes, the language of invasion and violence persists (2014, 2). Ironically, the social isolation, violence, and suicides attributed to the colonias can also be found in neighboring *fraccionamientos*.[3] Contravening these stereotypes becomes part of the colonia's campaign to legitimize their land claims. One way migrants combat this discourse is through documentation and the courts. In spite of popular narratives that consign Indigenous peoples to a violent past, Iván and Magda are modern subjects (Castellanos 2010a). They believe in formality and its bureaucracy, even if by living in a squat it appears otherwise. They purchased land from a private owner to avoid the problems of fraud and abuse associated with purchasing ejido land, where land titles may remain in dispute for decades. They have kept a meticulous record of their monthly payments. But since documentation is not enough, *colonos* turned to the courts.

Colonias as Spaces of Resistance

Much of the misery in shantytowns is the product of waiting, for the landowner to resolve land disputes and for the city to recognize squatters' rights. Caught between informal and formal bureaucracies, shantytown residents are stuck in limbo, always on the verge. As Auyero (2012) points out, acts of waiting become forms of domination, through which citizens are disciplined. Colonias are ideal sites to nurture political subordination, but they are also spaces known for insubordination. For Colonia Mario Villanueva, a fire motivated the residents of the colonia to construct a social movement.

On March 25, 2012, a parcel of land located next to the colonia that had become a clandestine neighborhood dump caught fire. The flames threatened several homes in the colonia, and residents had to be evacuated. When government officials arrived to assess the damage, they asked for proof of ownership. Residents showed them the receipts of their deposit and monthly payments provided by the landowner. The officials noticed several irregularities right away. First, the receipts were not official; some were handwritten. Second, the owner listed on the receipt was not the owner of the property. Third, the amounts listed as paid were inconsistent. The residents were informed that these irregularities placed them at risk of losing their homes. At first, they panicked. Then they mobilized.

The first shantytowns established in Cancún struggled with a lack of infrastructure. To advocate for improved services and regularization of land titles, residents formed grassroots organizations that were aligned with the PRI (McLean n.d.). Organizations like UCI and FUC quickly established a political base in Cancún. This type of organizing was not new in Colonia Mario Villanueva. Many *colonos* came from Indigenous pueblos with a long history of political organizing, including working with organizations like Antorcha Campesina. Founded in 1974 by professors and students from the Escuela Nacional de Agricultura, Antorcha joined forces with *campesinos* from the Mixteco community of Tecomatlán to improve access to education, health care, housing, and jobs.[4] It evolved into a national grassroots organization affiliated with the PRI that mobilized support for peasants' rights and more recently for urban residents and factory workers. This shift reflects Mexico's demographic trends. Mexico is becoming increasingly urban; a third of its Indigenous population resides in cities. As Antorcha expands its efforts to urban centers, Tecomatlán continues to serve as its model for organizing rural and urban communities.

Some of the *colonos* previously lived in colonias associated with UCI or FUC before moving to Mario Villanueva. Incidentally, the colonia's name is a direct reference to this type of political relationship. Mario Villanueva Madrid is a well-known PRI politician and agronomist, who was *presidente municipal* (1990–91) of Benito Juárez, the county seat where Cancún is located, before he became governor of Quintana Roo (1993–99). Accused of money laundering, he went into hiding before an arrest could be made at the end of his term as governor. When he was caught two years later, he was given a six-year prison sentence. Upon his release, he was extradited to the United States and given an eleven-year sentence for drug trafficking. In spite of these indictments, *colonos* commiserated with Villanueva's persecution by the Mexican and US governments and his own political party, and hailed his commitment to resolving land disputes and expanding Cancún's urban zone to include more irregular settlements. In the eyes of *colonos*, Villanueva's corruption is mitigated by his support for land regularization and squatter's rights. Naming the colonia after Villanueva reflects *colonos'* efforts to align themselves with folkloric heroes who championed colonia regularization, even as they rebuked his criminal history.

Soon after the fire, *colonos* met with the landowner to inform her of their refusal to make their monthly payments until she resolved the paperwork irregularities. Twenty-two residents took one step further. They filed a lawsuit against the landowner for fraud. They believed they had a strong case, but the lawyer they worked with was ineffectual in putting it together. In 2014, a judge ruled in favor of the landowner and permitted the expulsion of these families. These families were not reimbursed for the money they spent to purchase and improve their land parcels. Emboldened by this verdict, the landowner sued forty-two *colonos* for defaulting on their payments. *Colonos* perceived this action to be an act of retribution against those who were actively involved in protesting the eviction. Magda and Iván were included in this suit. Given the outcome of the first suit, *colonos* fear the court will most likely rule in the landowner's favor. In September 2014, with no support forthcoming from the municipal government or governor's office, Magda convinced her neighbors to reach out to Antorcha Campesina, which had recently broadened its rural origins to include *colonias populares*.

Magda first encountered Antorcha in her hometown of Sab'ak, where the organization worked with *ejidatarios*, including Magda's father, to advocate for maintaining communal land rights. At Magda's request, Antorcha sent two representatives to educate residents on their rights to property and dignity as Mexican citizens and to train them in how to mobilize a movement among the irregular settlements of Cancún. With Antorcha's aid, the residents organized mass marches and teach-ins, papered the city with fliers, mediated conversations with the landowner, and met with political representatives from the municipal and state governments. Antorcha mobilizes new urban settlers through a discourse of human rights and rights to property grounded in communal land rights. Antorcha representative David Sánchez Reyes explains that their project is fundamentally a "social project" intended to ameliorate the extreme poverty facing colonias. To address the severe housing shortage in Cancún, Antorcha purchased 8 hectares of land in 2008 that has been carved up into individual lots measuring 11 by 24 square meters and sold to its members at a price of Mex$8,500. Named Unión Antorchista, it serves as a social experiment to model social relations built on "neighborly trust" and communal participation.[5] If we ascribe to Donald Nonini's description of commons as "functioning arrangements that connect people to the material and social things they share and use to survive and operate outside of—but most frequently alongside—capitalist markets" (2006, 165), then Antorcha's new venture can be characterized as a social commons "organized around access by users to social resources created by specific kinds of [renewable] human labor" (166).

By bringing in advocates to rally on behalf of *colonos*, Antorcha Campesina made the colonia's concerns publicly visible and postponed the implementation of the court judgment. Although Antorcha is aligned with the PRI, the municipal government headed by the PRI (2013–16) treated the Antorchistas with caution, granting them meetings but making few promises or concessions. In negotiations that took place in January 2015, Antorcha entreated *colonos* to agree to pay Mex$80,000 for their plots with basic services included. The landowner countered by offering to sell the plots for Mex$160,000 without basic services, twice the price agreed upon in the original contract. Antorcha convinced *colonos* to accept this price but requested that basic services be included. *Colonos* would pay a deposit of Mex$30,000 (paid in three to four installments) and make monthly payments of 1,000 pesos over a period of eleven years. When the landowner balked at the request to include basic services, Antorcha reminded her that the new Law for Urban Development in Cancún requires that any landowner who wishes to parcel and sell lots for housing must provide basic services. Sánchez Reyes acknowledged that "what is detaining the negotiations is the price and the services." The landowner refused to negotiate further. The standstill has left the forty-two *colonos* in limbo. Their quest for a "dignified home" as promised to them by Article 4 in Mexico's constitution continues to be a struggle.

Witnessing an Eviction

The standstill did not hold. The landowner acted upon the legal judgement that gave her the authority to evict the twenty-two families involved in the first lawsuit. The eviction took place on a balmy afternoon in January 2015. I arrived in Colonia Mario Villanueva at four o'clock just as the eviction proceedings had begun. Magda had invited me and my five-year-old twins to eat tamales. I knew something was wrong when the main entrance to the colonia was blocked by a police truck. This entrance is accessible via a minor artery bordering the neighboring *fraccionamiento* of Villas Otoch. As I parked my car next to the police truck, I noticed a policeman leaning against the truck's hood, coolly observing a small crowd gathered at the entrance. Colonia residents were shouting and pleading at two unfamiliar figures, who yelled back. It was the landowner and the court representative waving a judicial order of eviction. They demanded that the twenty-two families listed on the eviction order gather their belongings and vacate their homes that afternoon. Magda was in the crowd. I could hear the desperation in the residents' pleas: they hadn't been forewarned. The timing was strategic. The Antorcha representatives were out of town, and the majority of the men in the colonia had just departed for work. As soon as she saw me, Magda asked me to intervene. She thought the landowner might listen to me, as a *gringa* and anthropologist. I pleaded their case to no avail. "Please leave, *señora*, or you will be forcibly removed along with the protesters," the court representative warned me. He informed everyone that the landowner was within her rights to enforce the eviction. The residents explained that many of the residents weren't at home to remove their belongings.

Within the hour, fifteen police trucks filled with one hundred policemen in full riot gear arrived to battle a crowd made up primarily of women and children. This show of force was intentional and disciplinary, sparking fear and calling forth specters of state violence with roots in settler colonial structures of dispossession. This violence is racialized and gendered because it strategically targets Indigenous women who are at the frontlines of land struggles. Jovana, Magda's cousin, and her kids, who were helping Magda make the tamales, had witnessed a violent eviction the year before. On this day, Jovana's seven-year-old daughter experienced flashbacks and started keening. At five years of age, my kids were too young to understand what was going on, but I feared for their safety. Magda was also concerned for her children's safety. Although Magda was not being threatened with eviction, she was one of the leaders of the protest and needed to stay to impede the evictions. She couldn't leave the colonia to pick up her children from school. I volunteered to meet them and drop them off at Jovana's house, which was located in a neighboring settlement. By this time, the police had begun to barricade the main exit with their trucks to prevent people from leaving and entering the colonia. Accompanied by Jovana and her family, my children and I quickly jumped into my car and drove past the barricade. Before we departed, I pleaded with one of the policemen to treat the residents with respect because they were good people. "I always do," he replied, "but I can't speak for my *compañeros*." I was stunned by the massive state power deliberately engaged in the service of private property to politically repress migrant families, especially women and children.

After escorting the children to Jovana's house, I planned to return to the colonia. However, Magda notified us that by six o'clock the police, intent on containing the protesters and preventing them from seeking additional support, had locked down the colonia. The electricity was shut off and no one was allowed to enter or leave, even residents who lived there, until the early hours the following morning. To mitigate the violence on women, children, and the elderly, Magda and her coleaders contacted their male relatives, who joined their efforts to stop the demolition and protect *colonos* from the police. During the scuffle with the police, several people were injured, including a pregnant woman. A demolition crane flattened all twenty-two houses. When Magda walked me through the devastation, she shared stories of the displaced families. As she pointed out the remains of neighbors' homes, debris scattered everywhere, it almost felt like a parody of an archaeological tour. But it was a different kind of tour from the ones most *gringas* seek out in Cancún.

The next day the residents headed straight for the governor's office to protest against police brutality and the evictions, and request restitution for damaged property. A few months later, Antorcha organized a mass protest held strategically on the fifth of May, a day that commemorates the victory of a small Mexican army battalion over French imperial forces (fig. 9). Hundreds of protestors demanded affordable housing and a halt to evictions in colonias Mario Villanueva and El Fortín. They marched through

FIGURE 9. Antorcha Campesina protest. Photograph by author.

downtown Cancún and held rallies in front of the *ayuntamiento* (municipal government headquarters) and the governor's office.

The Commons as Critique

Antorcha's long campaign to end the evictions in Colonia Mario Villanueva had mixed results. On the one hand, Antorcha's petitions prompted government officials to meet with colonia residents after the eviction. The government offered concessions like warm blankets and food supplies, even paving the colonia's main road with gravel. Since it was an election year, a large banner stating "Work brigades with results" was posted next to the paved road to publicize this promise fulfilled (fig. 10). Ironically, the banner was also placed in front of a demolished house, underscoring settler violence at work. Most of the families in the colonia were unable to maintain the level of political action requested by Antorcha Campesina, especially after the organization, beginning in March 2017, organized a three-month sit-in in front of the municipal palace to protest the violent eviction of *colonos* from the Colonia El Fortín. Magda participated in the first month of the sit-in, dedicating twenty hours per week to this effort, but she withdrew

FIGURE 10. Campaign slogan "Work brigades with results." Photograph by author.

when it became too difficult to care for her newborn infant. By removing herself from the campaign, Magda lost her right to claim membership in Antorcha. In May 2017, when Antorcha persuaded the new municipal government run by the Green Ecologist Party of Mexico (Partido Verde Ecologista de México or PVEM) to agree to provide new plots with titles, only twelve of the families in Colonia Mario Villanueva were included in this overture. In her study of informal settlements in Mexico City, Ann Varley (2017) found that titling is more likely than not to result in displacement.

As the date for the judgment in Magda's court case approached, the landowner doubled the asking price to Mex$320,000 per parcel and put up the twenty-two lots for sale. Sensing a victory against the forty-two families named in her suit, the landowner's threats of eviction were palpable. I asked Iván and Magda why they didn't abandon the colonia and move to a *fraccionamiento*. After working in Cancún's hotel industry for over a decade, Iván has accrued enough points in his INFONAVIT account to purchase a home in a social housing development. "Because you can't live well," he replied. As David Harvey observes, "it is the failure of individualized private property rights to fulfill our common interests in the way they are supposed to do" (2011, 104). In spite of the precarity of the shantytown, Iván and Magda value the sense of community nurtured by *colonos*. They know every family in the colonia. They share meals, watch each other's children, march alongside each other, rally for justice, and debate the future. Informal settlements are organized like ejidos, communal landholdings that function like a commons of shared land and resources intended to benefit the community as a whole. Lacking support from the state, *colonos* share and pool scarce resources with the intent of creating self-sustaining and politically organized communities. Fifty-two percent of land in Mexico is held in common (Robson and Lichtenstein 2013). Maya people participate in the largest number of ejidos (1,019 *comunidades* and ejidos making up the largest area—5,343,576 hectares) in Mexico (Klooster 2013). The commons represents a dominant model for social organizing, especially for Maya migrants. By invoking the commons, the colonia is transformed into a public and material manifestation of these ideals—of shared resources and collective decision making—in an urban setting, especially in a world where urbanization and privatization increasingly threaten the commons (Robson and Lichtenstein 2013).

In contrast, *fraccionamientos* are notorious for their lack of community and sense of alienation, which has been exacerbated by a spate of foreclosures (Inclán-Valadez 2013; Monkkonen 2018). To address these concerns, INFONAVIT established the nonprofit organization Fundación Hogares, whose main goal is to produce projects promoting community solidarity. Yet, in Mexico, living well has become increasingly tied with tract housing. Efforts are being made to reconfigure these developments to improve overcrowding and provide onsite maintenance, but the changes have not resolved problems of internal violence and crime stemming from housing overproduction and privatization's focus on individualization and capital accumulation (Fuentes and Hernandez 2014). For the residents of Colonia Mario Villanueva, precarity is preferable to this type of social anomie. Not surprisingly, Magda and Iván purchased another lot in a new colonia located on the outskirts of the city's urban plan. Iván's cousins purchased the neighboring lots. The landowner provided a formal written contract, but the colonia lacks basic services. Magda and Iván will need to wait for the government to incorporate and regulate this new colonia, but in the meantime, they will be surrounded by family and by a community that values land and advocates collectively for social justice and autonomy. As Michi Saagiig Nishnaabeg scholar Leanne Betasamosake Simpson (2017) attests, "*how* we live, *how* we organize, *how* we engage the world—the process—not only frames the outcome, it is the transformation. *How* molds and then gives birth to the present. The *how* changes us. *How* is the theoretical intervention. Engaging in deep and reciprocal Indigeneity is a transformative act because it fundamentally changes modes of production of our lives. It changes the relationships that house our bodies and our thinking."

A Cautionary Tale
of Indebtedness

THIS FRAMED IMAGE took pride of place on the living room wall of
doña Clara's two-room concrete block home (fig. 11). Magazine clippings
of twelve beautiful homes had been pasted on a simple wood frame. The
homes are stately and spacious, adorned with stone fountains, reflecting
pools, and extensive manicured lawns. This montage evokes the dream
of homeownership. Because this dream is compelling and marketable,
it has been promoted as a universal dream that is desired by everyone,
despite its ties to the historical, economic, and racial conditions in the
United States that first gave rise to this ideal and that continue to perpet-
uate it (see Kwak 2015). Homeownership is perceived as the path toward
wealth, self-sufficiency, and liberal citizenship. Ironically, what is elided
from this narrative is the infrastructure holding it up; implementing this
dream on a mass scale requires government subsidies. For example, the
quintessential suburban town of Levittown was built with federal loans,
while the GI Bill funded mortgages for white families (Katznelson 2005).[1]
In Latin America, the dream of homeownership has been reimagined to
encompass government-subsidized social housing developments like Paseos
Kabah—scaled-down versions of suburbia that are marketed as affordable
and "green." These projects continue to idealize a white, heteronormative
nuclear family and to frame suburban housing as "modern," as a sign of
national progress, regardless of high vacancy rates, loan defaults, and rising
insecurity.[2] Homeownership reflects a settler colonial fantasy of whiteness,
a racialized and gendered story of indebtedness and dispossession where, as
Fred Moten suggests, "the financialization of everyday life was a plantation

FIGURE 11. Settler dream of housing. Photograph by author.

[and settler colonial] imposition" (2013, 240; See 2012).³ After the onset of
the 2008 global housing collapse, critics rebuked this dream because it was
based on debt and on intentionally steering the working class and communities of color toward subprime loans (Stiglitz 2010). But as Moten argues,
"the discourse of social development has always been subprime" (2013, 240).
Predatory practices of dispossession are derived from settler technologies.
The ownership society and subprime lending are exclusionary practices
intentionally organized around the negation of Black and Indigenous lives
and their dispossession (Moten 2013). As such, it behooves us to account
for how settler colonial fantasies of ownership have been deployed to reorder
Indigenous lives in Latin America and how Indigenous communities are
resisting these impositions.

Doña Clara's montage of aspirational homes draws attention to the
artifice upholding this illusion of wealth, security, and national belonging.
She created this montage to serve as an inspiration board while she built
her house on a plot of land given to her by her son-in-law Horacio (introduced in chapter 2). The plot was carved out of an ejido land grant that had
been subdivided after agrarian reform and sold to migrants like Horacio,

before it was transferred to doña Clara's keeping. "This is my dream," said doña Clara to explain why she created the montage. At first glance the two-room concrete block house she built does not look anything like the photographs that hang on her wall. But as Janet Carsten and Stephen Hugh-Jones (1995) remind us, the house is more than an architectural structure; it is an embodiment of social and economic relations that shift over time and space. Doña Clara's concrete block house reflects these intangible and entangled histories. Situated on ejido land, it is a physical manifestation of an ideological shift in property regimes, from a tradition of collective land ownership to liberal notions of individual property rights. Her rights to her plot are informal; she will not be granted the title of her plot until she pays it off, thus highlighting the unevenness of this transformation. For doña Clara, this plot encapsulates a dream of self-sufficiency that she was unable to achieve until she was in her early fifties, and that pushes beyond prescribed gender roles and state expectations. A house of her own makes her economically independent from her ex-husband whose troubles with alcoholism contributed to years of financial instability and mental anguish. It is the culmination of decades of toiling as a maid and cleaner and struggling to survive the ebbs and flows of a fickle tourism industry.

Doña Clara's montage also speaks to the national push to move away from land and instead impose a mortgaged house, in the form of tract housing, as the dominant symbol by which to imagine national belonging in Mexico. In Cancún, the traditional *palapa* is being displaced from the landscape by thousands of suburban townhomes. In the process, the history of Cancún as an Indigenous space is erased and paved over by a suburban imaginary. As Cancún celebrates its fiftieth anniversary, it reckons with what this means for a city that has relied on a Mexican tradition of simultaneously exalting and erasing an Indigenous past while denying and disparaging an Indigenous present and future.

Coda

Eight years after they defaulted on their loan, Mariela and Francisco ran out of time. They were evicted from their home on July 25, 2018. That morning they were awakened by a pounding on their door. Groggy with sleep, Mariela and Francisco were shocked to be handed a judicial order of eviction by a local judge, who was accompanied by an HSBC bank representative, a team of movers, and four municipal police officers. Prior to this eviction, the British-based HSBC bank had acquired Francisco's loan from Tertius. "They entered our house and began to pressure us to leave. 'You have to leave or we will forcibly remove you,'" Francisco recalled them saying. Mariela's first thought was "Where are we going to go?" Francisco immediately called the lawyer managing his case. "He told me it was all legal. In that moment you can't do anything. You feel this great pressure and you can't do anything. You feel frustrated. Impotent." The presence of the police, dressed in riot gear and armed with guns, alarmed them. "They told us that if we didn't leave, they would enter our house, beat us. By hook or crook, we will be removed," Mariela grimly explained. In the space of one hour, their lives changed. As the movers began packing up their belongings, they joined them to ensure everything made it on the moving truck. It took them one day to pack up a life. Fortunately, Mariela's sister invited them to move in with her, giving them somewhere to go. "The bank doesn't care if you have no place to go," Francisco angrily recounted. "It doesn't care if your children don't have anything to eat. It doesn't care of you aren't working. It doesn't care if you are sick. None of that matters. You're out no matter what." The bank representative and court official stood by and watched the entire time. Neighbors stopped by in solidarity, to denounce the injustice of it all.

The eviction took place three weeks after Andrés Manuel López Obrador was elected president of Mexico. The transition period between an election and inauguration day is a time of great chaos, with ousted public officials jumping ship, while programs and projects languish or speed up before the new administration steps in. In Quintana Roo, the National Regeneration Movement (Movimiento Regeneración Nacional or MORENA) party won municipal and national elections, while the governorship remained in the hands of the PAN. In light of López Obrador's populist bent, companies like Tertius sped up foreclosure proceedings. A year later, López Obrador did demand that INFONAVIT and FOVISSSTE end evictions, which they agreed to do in February 2020.[4] In Paseos Kabah during the month of July 2018, foreclosures took place daily. After the eviction, Francisco filed countersuits, fervently hoping they might be able to recoup something, if not the house, especially since he continued to pay his INFONAVIT loan. During discovery, Francisco's lawyer learned that INFONAVIT had ceded its rights to HSBC, leaving the bank as the sole backer of Francisco's loan and capable of proceeding with eviction.

When Francisco's suit was denied by a judge and his lawyer told him to give up, Francisco sought other lawyers. One lawyer told him to wise up: "You messed with the government. There's nothing you can do." But another lawyer proposed Francisco form an association of debtors to fight the bank. "We can fight as a group," explained Francisco. "I wanted to reproduce the dynamics of the *pueblo* [ejido community of Kuchmil]. The majority of the people in the pueblo are fighters and workers. In the pueblo, they fight, and everyone has something." Francisco recruited ten families evicted from Paseos Kabah to form this association, but soon after they made their first deposit, the lawyer ghosted them. Francisco pulled up the texts the lawyer sent him to show me when they stopped. Looking forlorn, he ponders if there is a way to publicly shame him. Francisco acknowledged that claiming Indigenous rights in a city is a daunting task. "Things are different in the city. To exercise my [Indigenous] rights, I have to go to [Kuchmil]. The rights pertain to the pueblo to which you belong. Here we don't have any representation. How can you fight [without representation]?" A year after the eviction, they conceded defeat. Mariela regrets that they were evicted before the López Obrador administration stepped in. "Maybe we wouldn't have lost our house."

When Mariela and Francisco shared this tragic story with me in January of 2020, they looked defeated, but they declared they were "at peace" with their predicament. When I met with them in February of 2018, they had been optimistic of finding a way to stave off eviction, if not avoid it altogether. But now their slumped shoulders and the tears in their eyes told a different story. The humiliation of being evicted was compounded by job loss and health catastrophes. Francisco suffered from depression and had a difficult time controlling his diabetes, leading to the loss of a big toe six months after the eviction. Mariela's blood pressure skyrocketed, and she has since developed ovarian cysts. "I try to stay calm, to not show how angry I am, because it doesn't help him to worry and he thinks about it too much." She quit her job to help care for her husband after his operation. With the help of Francisco's sister, who is a nurse, they were able to help him heal. Francisco can no longer work as a waiter. He can't walk very far without feeling pain and is working to regain his balance. Mariela has returned to work as a domestic servant to make ends meet.

Mariela's sister and her family helped them get through this painful period, especially since they were never blessed with children of their own. Living with boisterous children has kept them from falling into a deep depression. It also gave them time to save money to build a house on a lot Francisco had purchased through a *traspaso* in a neighboring *región* in 2002. The lot came up for sale because it was difficult to build on; a deep depression took up half of the lot. Francisco rented out the rustic *palapa* that came with the plot to cover the monthly payments; it was paid in full two years ago. When they defaulted on their loan, Francisco gifted the lot to Mariela (who had not cosigned the loan), which prevented the lot from being confiscated by Tertius and gave them a backup plan in case of eviction. In December 2019 they moved into a newly constructed *palapa*, painted mint green. "It's nothing like our house," Mariela exclaimed wistfully when she showed me her kitchen. The narrow galley kitchen is tiny and decorated with white wallpaper covered in bright green cacti. The living room doubles as a bedroom, while the front portico serves as a dining room. Unlike most *palapas*, they installed cement floors (instead of dirt) and had the bathroom plumbed with a shower, flushable toilet, and sink. The place bears Mariela's stamp—tidy, extremely clean, and well organized.

INFONAVIT had ceded its right to collect on the loan to HSBC, but since the house had not yet sold, Francisco's INFONAVIT loan was still current and on the books. When Francisco stopped working, INFONAVIT demanded he continue to pay his loan, even though the house no longer belonged to him. Since the hotel where Francisco worked had shut down in response to a labor strike, INFONAVIT was unable to garnish Francisco's wages. "I had to ask for a document from Mexico [City] to cancel the loan," explained Francisco. INFONAVIT did end up canceling the loan. INFONAVIT's actions are reflective of the underhanded and predatory tactics characteristic of subprime lending and the settler logic of dispossession.

Despite these tragic events, Francisco remains optimistic. Mariela thinks they are better off. "Initially, after living in a beautiful house, to move to a *palapita* with a leaky roof, I was incredibly sad. But this is our reality. But now it's a good thing that this is our land. No one can take it away because it's mine. We won't be renting for the rest of our lives. We have a place to belong."

Right before the national elections, two other Maya migrants from Kuchmil went into foreclosure. They had paired an INFONAVIT loan with a mortgage from a SOFOL. As they wait it out, they too have been exposed to the disciplinary tactics of foreclosure. But López Obrador's mandate to end foreclosures has given them hope.

Meanwhile, Magda and Iván have managed to stay in the colonia. The lawsuit has yet to resolve itself. "The *colonos* who purchased the lots [that formerly belonged to the twenty-two families who were evicted in 2012] are making things difficult for the landowner," Magda explained when I visited her in January 2020. "One of the *colonos*, her nephew is a lawyer. He looked at her contract and told her it was not legally binding. They have all built houses made of concrete block. To protect these houses, they are suing the landowner." Facing a new lawsuit accusing her of fraud, the landowner has backed off evicting the forty-two families named in the lawsuit she filed in 2014. With the advent of a new political party in the municipal office, the landowner has lost the support she was granted by previous administrations. Magda and Iván are waiting it out, though they could decamp to the plot they purchased a few years ago on the outskirts of Cancún, where they recently built a one-room concrete block house. "We're still here and don't plan on leaving."

Regroundings

The shift from land to house entails a "regrounding" of the meanings of "home" that "pays close attention to specific processes, modes and materialities . . . in different contexts and on different scales" (Ahmed et al. 2003, 2). Social housing provides an example of this regrounding and the intimate, relational, and dynamic aspects of home making (Carsten and Hugh-Jones 1995). These housing units have become symbolic of whiteness, as evidenced by the pervasive billboards of light-skinned nuclear families living the good life. They have also come to signify "progress," cementing Mexico's transformation into a modern nation-state. Maya migrants consider these homes to be "modern," marking a distinct temporal, material, and spatial shift from rural to urban living, from *campesino* to urban proletariat. The size of these homes and plots make it difficult to accommodate multigenerational households and gardens. Social housing is an assimilative experience because it *financializes* Indigenous lives in pernicious ways. This is the reordering to which Moten (2013) refers.

To maximize profits, social housing units are built on the smallest plots possible. These units take up much of the land available, leaving tiny strips of green space and thus making the land seem inconsequential to housing. Prioritizing the house structure diverts our attention away from another facet of settler colonialism—land expropriation. The historical divestment of land from racialized minorities is a central tenet of settler colonialism. Under US settler colonialism, African Americans and Native Americans have lost thousands of acres of property (Cronon 1983; Daniel 2015; Taylor 2019).[5] In Mexico, neoliberal policies such as NAFTA have escalated Indigenous land loss. While Cancún's unprecedented expansion has been considered an example of tourism run amok, it is also predicated on the expropriation of Indigenous lands. The development of thousands of hectares for social housing is a direct outcome of land encroachment and predatory lending. As Maya migrants engage with this new type of homeownership, they grapple with the shifting meanings of debt and with the way land and nature are being reimagined as property, as something that can be possessed and sold. The financialization of Cancún's housing market has made them even more vulnerable to the vagaries of global financial markets and tourism economies, placing them at risk of being dispossessed.

At the same time, these processes of financialization and extraction are producing new radical agents—Indigenous homeowners. This juxtaposition of Indigenous with homeowner disorients and denaturalizes settler colonial and colonial tropes of the rural Indian that erase Indigenous peoples from urban landscapes. Indigenous homeowners like Mariela and Francisco are political and historical agents, shaped by a long history of Maya dispossession and struggles for autonomy. Life in Cancún disciplines Indigenous migrants to pull away from land tenure practices rooted in the ejido to imagine new ways of relating to home, land, the built environment, and each other. For Maya migrants, however, the neoliberal push toward individual indebtedness recalls a history of Indigenous dispossession and thus necessitates a reworking of the cautionary tale of *esclavitud* for this new era of financialization. By evoking *esclavitud* in an urban context, this cautionary tale critiques the settler logics that have erased indigeneity from Cancún's foundational fictions and urban landscape. It is a critique of social housing that has expropriated ejido land to convert it into a miniaturized version of the settler dream of homeownership. It is also a critique of the collusion between state and capital to dispossess Indigenous people of their lands, their homes, and their dignity. And it is a critique of state-sanctioned gender violence. To resist these efforts, Maya migrants draw upon a history of Indigenous resistance to wait out the state and capital. Waiting out becomes an Indigenous temporality that disrupts the logic of dispossession and converts waiting into an act of insubordination. In so doing, they construct an alternative approach to financialization that regrounds their ties to home and land based on rural traditions and Indigenous practices.

Indigenous homeowners like Magda and Iván disrupt assimilationist development narratives that deracialize Indigenous people when they move to urban centers. Instead, they demand to be recognized as Indigenous in urban spaces. Although Article 2 of the constitution recognizes Indigenous peoples' rights to self-determination, these customary practices are associated with territorial rights in rural communities, with jurisdiction restricted to the municipal level, even as the privatization of the ejido is leading to Indigenous dispossession (Seider 2002). This legal framework uplifts cultural rights over land rights, to the detriment of Indigenous women, who remain excluded from land redistribution (Altamirano-Jiménez 2017). Bettina Ng'weno (2012) shows that for Afro-Colombians, demands for substantive citizenship are hindered by a legal divide that associates autonomy with rural spaces and racial discrimination with urban spaces. As Glen Coulthard suggests, a colonial politics of recognition is *"a field of power through which colonial relations are produced and maintained"* (2014, 17). As such, state recognition of Indigenous rights does not necessarily translate into meaningful reciprocity, but instead ends up reproducing racialized and gendered colonial power dynamics (e.g., Ng'weno 2007). In Mexico, we see this play out in the ways Indigenous *pueblos* are treated as fixed entities. Since the right to self-determination is not conceptualized as an urban experience, state and municipal governments engage with Indigenous pueblos as rural, as territorially bound. But once Indigenous people move to cities like Cancún, they are no longer perceived to be Indigenous. Rather, Indigenous people are treated as deracialized subjects. As a consequence, they are not granted the full rights as Indigenous people and as citizens with the right to a dignified life, and continue to bear the brunt of state violence in service to settler capitalism.

As Bettina Ng'weno (2012) shows, Indigenous and Afro-Latin Americans' claims to autonomy and territory are transforming ideas of citizenship. Galvanized by the parallels between their ancestors' struggle with *esclavitud* and their own land and housing struggles, Maya migrants demand to be engaged as Indigenous and accorded the rights to land and self-determination. Migrants like Magda and Iván urge us to engage with a more expansive conception of territoriality, one that is not limited to the land boundaries of rural communities but is broad enough to recognize the peninsula's sacred Maya geography and to encompass Indigenous diasporas in urban centers. Through this articulation, they offer a more dynamic interpretation of Indigenous rights that aims to combat settler tactics of elimination through assimilation and dispossession. In so doing, Maya migrants are forging a new vision of Indigenous urbanism that moves beyond a colonial politics of recognition.

Abbreviations

CNBV	National Banking and Securities Commission
CONDUSEF	National Commission for the Protection and Defense of Users of Financial Services
CORETT	Committee for the Regulation of Land Tenure
DIF	National System for Integral Family Development
FONATUR	National Fund for the Development of Tourism
FONACOT	National Fund for Worker Consumption
FOVIMI	Housing Fund for the Military
FOVISSSTE	Social Security Institute's Housing Fund for Federal Government Employees
FUC	Only Settlers' Front
Su Casita	Hipotecaria Su Casita
IFC	International Finance Corporation
INCO	National Institute for the Consumer
INFONAVIT	National Institute for Funding Workers' Housing
INFOVIR	Institute for the Development of Housing and Property Regularization
INVIQROO	Housing Institute of the State of Quintana Roo
IPAE	Institute of State Patrimony

MORENA	National Regeneration Movement
NAFTA	North American Free Trade Agreement
PAN	National Action Party
PRI	Institutional Revolutionary Party
PROFECO	Office of the Federal Prosecutor for the Consumer
SOFOL	Financial Society of Limited Scope
SOFOM	Financial Society of Multiple Scope
SEDUVI	Ministry of Urban Development and Housing
SHF	Federal Mortgage Society
UCI	Union of Independent Settlers
UDI	Unit of Account

Notes

Introduction

1. Doris Sommer (1993) coined the term "foundational fictions" to explain how modern heterosexual romance became aligned with patriotic ideals of nationalism. I loosely apply Sommer's term because it captures the idea of mythic nation building. While ideas of conquest have been tied to heterosexual romance, I do not make this claim for the case of Cancún.

2. For a more detailed discussion of Cancún as a tourist pole, see Clancy 1991.

3. The Maya center is also spelled *cah*. For a historical overview of Tihó, see Restall 1997. For an overview of the precolonial sites in Quintana Roo, see C. J. Walker 2009 and Shaw and Matthews 2005.

4. The spelling of the island has varied. Carlos Plank, who served as Interim Governor of the Federal Territory of Quintana Roo during 1915–16, spelled it "Cancum" (Macías Richard 1997, 259). Martí refers to the island as "Kankún" and "Kan Kún" (1991, 18). The place of the accent over the letter "u" also varies. Martí (1991), for example, does not use an accent in his book title. I adopt the spelling used by the city—Cancún. When I do deviate from this spelling, I do so because I am citing authors who rely on a different spelling of this name.

5. Maya ruins in Quintana Roo were surveyed in the mid-1950s, but the INAH's Regional Center of the Southeast (Centro Regional del Sureste) did not begin a substantial study of these sites until the 1970s. See Con Uribe 2005.

6. The first museum, Museo Arqueológico de Cancún, was built in 1982 as part of the Convention Center. In 2012, this museum was replaced with the much larger and grander Museo Maya de Cancún in the Zona Hotelera.

7. Martí describes the Territory of Quintana Roo as "the furthest and most forbidding area of the nation" (1991, 7).

8. Over one-third, 38.67 percent, of the residents of the municipality of Benito Juárez, where Cancún is located, identify as Indigenous (Encuesta Intercensal 2015).

9. For these descriptions, see Redclift 2005, 84 and Martí 1991. For a discussion of the computer algorithm story, see Robert Dunphy, "Why the Computer Chose Cancún," *New York Times*, March 5, 1972.

10. See Castellanos 2017.

11. For a discussion of settler colonialism in Latin America, see Castellanos 2017.

12. Laura Harjo (2019) has developed "way-finding tools" to help Indigenous communities envision their own futurity.

13. Recent archaeological research using LiDAR shows that Maya city-states were more complex and densely populated than previously documented. See Tom Clynes, "Exclusive: Laser Scans Reveal Maya 'Megalopolis' below Guatemalan Jungle," *National Geographic*, February 1, 2018, https://news.nationalgeographic.com/2018/02/maya-laser-lidar-guatemala -pacunam/.

14. Maya peoples have participated in migration before, during, and after colonialism. For a discussion of migration during colonialism, see Farriss 1984. For a discussion of migration during the early national period, see Rugeley 1996. And for a discussion of migration in contemporary times, see Castellanos 2010a.

15. I rely on David Harvey's definition of neoliberalism: "a theory of political economic practices that proposes that human well-being can best be advanced by liberating individual entrepreneurial freedoms and skills within an institutional framework characterized by strong private property rights, free markets, and free trade" (2005, 2).

16. For decolonial guides of other cities, like Los Angeles, Chicago, and Minneapolis, see "Mapping Indigenous LA," https://mila.ss.ucla.edu/; "Settler Colonial City Project," https://settlercolonialcityproject.org/; and "Connect with Mni Sota Makoce, an Indigenous Place," https://mnhum.org/native-nations-minnesota/.

17. These reforms expand upon previous efforts by the Mexican government to promote homeownership. Since the 1960s, housing policies for the working poor have focused on self-built housing, rental housing, public housing, and social housing (Bredenoord and Montiel 2014; A. Gilbert 1993; Gilbert and Ward 1985; Hartman forthcoming; Ward, Jiménez Huerta, and Di Virgilio 2015). Social housing commonly refers to rental housing made available at subsidized rates to low-income families by the government or other organizations (Hansson and Lundgren 2019). In Mexico, social housing encompasses both rental housing and housing finance subsidies. Social housing (also referred to as social interest housing) emerged in Mexico in the early 1900s and was directed toward developing public housing for the proletariat (Schwanse 2014). By the 1970s, social housing had expanded to include housing credits for home purchases, following the establishment of INFONAVIT. After 2000, social housing was oriented primarily toward housing finance subsidies and loans, leading to the mass construction of tract housing (Bredenoord and Cabrera Montiel 2014).

18. I use pseudonyms for rural villages here, with the exception of large towns and cities.

19. For a discussion of ejidos as sustainable ecologies, see Mike Gaworecki, "Mexico's ejidos are finding greater sustainability by involving youth and women," Mongabay Series: Indigenous Peoples and Conservation, June 2018, https://news.mongabay.com/2018/06 /mexicos-ejidos-are-finding-greater-sustainability-by-involving-youth-and-women/.

20. For a discussion of the politics of returning again and again to a particular place and the ethics of representation, see Castellanos 2019.

21. The term *criollo* refers to a Spaniard who was born in the Americas, whereas the term *creole* refers to a person of African or Indian (from the subcontinent) descent.

22. See Herzog (2013). *Repartimiento* was the system of conscripted Indigenous labor that was employed throughout the colonial period in Latin America. The *encomienda* system was a "restricted and well-defined institution in which the holder [of the land] performed certain government duties and in return received tribute [from Indigenous peoples] which residually belonged to the crown" (Lockhart and Schwartz 1983, 94). Although the encomienda system was abolished by royal decree in 1718, the *encomienda* prevailed in Yucatán until 1785 (Farriss 1984).

23. See Castro and Picq 2017 and Tuori 2015.

24. The works of Smith 2012 and Coulthard 2014 have been groundbreaking.

25. For the exceptions, see Gott 2007 and Salvatorre 2008.

26. Also see Speed 2017.

27. The hacienda was a private estate dedicated to ranching or agricultural production. During colonial Yucatán, haciendas concentrated on cattle ranching and the cultivation of corn, which required a "mild labor system" (G. Joseph 1988, 20). By the late eighteenth century, haciendas turned to henequen cultivation, although some specialized in sugar, cotton, tobacco, and rice. Henequen cultivation was labor intensive and led to an upsurge in debt peonage among Indigenous *campesinos*, transforming the hacienda into a plantation system (G. Joseph 1988).

28. Peasants also came from Campeche, Yucatán, Veracruz, Puebla, Guerrero, Morelos, Oaxaca, Distrito Federal, Hidalgo, Jalisco, Sinaloa, and Sonora (Collier 1994).

29. For a discussion of cities as sites for identity conflicts, see Davis and Libertun de Duren 2011.

30. For thinking through new planes of difference, including, for example, moving beyond human/nature distinctions, see Escobar 2018 and Marisol de la Cadena 2018, "Uncommons," Theorizing the Contemporary, *Fieldsights*, March 29, https://culanth.org/fieldsights/uncommons.

31. See Stiglitz 2013; Stout 2016a, 2016b; Warren and Warren Tyagi 2007.

32. See for example, Forrest and Yip 2013; Lopez 2015; Murphy 2015; and Zavisca 2012. Studies of housing in Latin America examine squatters and the rise of shantytowns (M. Davis 2006; Fischer et al. 2014; A. Gilbert 1993; A. Gilbert and Ward 1995; Penglase 2014), crime and insecurity (Caldeira 2001; Goldstein 2004; Moodie 2012), and urban middle-class enclaves and shopping malls (Dávila 2012; Dinzey-Flores 2013).

33. For an overview of Mexico's housing policies, see Bredenoord and Cabrera Montiel 2014; Gilbert and Varley 1991; and Hartman 2017, forthcoming.

34. The 40 percent figure is from 2000.

35. Author notes from Sebastián Fernández Cortina, "Housing in Practice" Roundtable, "Housing Across Borders: Mexico and U.S. Housing in Perspective" Symposium, Center for U.S.-Mexican Studies, UC San Diego School of Global Policy and Strategy, May 26, 2017.

36. President López Obrador instituted reforms to end evictions, provide mortgage loans for same-sex couples, and restructure fees. See "¿Tienes un crédito Infonavit?, AMLO propone cambios que te interesan," *Expansión*, June 18, 2019, https://expansion.mx/finanzas-personales/2019/06/18/tienes-un-credito-infonavit-amlo-propone-cambios-que-te-interesan.

Chapter One

1. The term citizen can evoke membership in a multitude of spaces—those territorially bounded (e.g., the nation-state, states within nations, and cities) or imagined (e.g., transnational communities) (Holston and Appadurai 1999). Through the use of the term *citizen*, I aim to evoke both types of belonging. Since I am discussing the movement and displacement of people as they cross state lines within a settler nation-state, I am concerned here with understanding how citizenship is interpreted not only by the nation-state (here deployed through state institutions), but also by migrants themselves as they participate in multiple spaces of belonging. I engage with James Holston and Arjun Appadurai's call to examine the disjunctures caused by the tension between formal and substantive citizenship (1999, 4–5).

2. See Farriss 1984; Martí 1991; Reed 1964; and Rugeley 1996.

3. For a discussion of Indigenous migrants as settlers, see Gutiérrez Nájera and Maldonado 2017.

4. For discussions of rural Mexican women's property rights, see Baitenmann 1997; Botey 1998; Deere and León de Leal 2001, 2002; González Montes 1988; Robichaux 1988; and Stephen 1997. For a discussion of how formalization impacts women's rights to rural and urban property, see Varley 2007.

5. For further discussion on rural women's rights to property after *ejido* reform, see Baitenmann 1997; Botey 1998; Deere and León de Leal 2001, 2002; Stephen 1996, 1997; Villagómez and Pinto 1997.

6. Although globalization processes highlight the constructed nature of the nation-state as an ideological project that is no longer geographically bound (Abrams 1988), Trouillot (2001) and Gupta (1995) call attention to its concreteness. Gupta shows that the Indian state is made visibly tangible by ethnographically tracing the discourses of corruption in the media and the practices of corruption among local bureaucratic officials.

7. For a detailed discussion of the relationship between kin-mediated migration networks and regional economies, see Wilson 1993.

8. This room forms part of the irregular housing market in Cancún. The government does not have the manpower to regulate the construction of secondary buildings on private property, even if the land was acquired through a government housing agency. For further discussion on the relationships between landlords and renters, see Gilbert and Varley 1991.

9. The exchange rate for the Mexican peso in 1998 was eleven pesos to one US dollar. In 2000, the average exchange rate was 9.2 pesos to one dollar. In 2004, the average exchange rate was 10.94 pesos to one dollar.

10. Migrants allot their daily salary toward housing and rely on tips to cover other expenses. In 2001 during the high season, hotel and discotheque employees earned US$100–US$200 a month in tips, but during the low season, tips diminished substantially to as low as US$50 a month.

11. Leonardo moved for a number of reasons. The first move was due to the need for better housing. The second move was a result of Horacio's getting married; after Horacio moved into a room on his father-in-law's property, Leonardo and his roommate moved into a smaller room. However, in spite of this move, their housing expenses remained high. Eventually, Leonardo moved into the home of his other brother and his family. After a year and a half, Leonardo moved to a more central location in town, which he shared with a friend from Kuchmil. In 2001, he moved again because he lived too far from the bus route to his new job.

12. These units were sold by private developers and were not built with government contracts. They were not social housing units.

13. The price for *terrenos baldíos* varies. *Ejidatarios* determine the price of the land, the deposit required, and the number and amount of monthly payments. I include a range of the prices Maya migrants paid for this type of property.

14. After World War II, the industrialization of urban centers in developing countries attracted a steady stream of people from the countryside. This rural-to-urban migration resulted in the development of irregular settlements (Ward 1982). To address this housing crisis and promote social-interest housing, the Mexican government established three federally-funded public agencies in 1972: INFONAVIT, FOVISSSTE, and the Housing Fund for the Military (Fondo de la Vivienda Militar or FOVIMI) (Gilbert and Varley 1991). INFONAVIT caters to workers employed in the private sector by offering home loans through a lending institution funded by employer contributions; employers contribute 5 percent of their employees' daily wages as credit toward this program (www.infonavit.gob.mx). FOVISSSTE provides home loans for government employees and their families (www.fovissste.gob.mx). FOVIMI finances housing for military employees.

15. Other states established similar housing institutes, like the Instituto de la Vivienda (Housing Institute or INVI) in Mexico City and the Instituto de la Vivienda de Oaxaca (Housing Institute of Oaxaca or INVO).

16. Interview with Architect Martín Martínez, then INVIQROO's director, February 21, 2002.

17. Interview with Edgar Campos García, representative of INVIQROO, November 16, 2000.

18. *Ejidatarios* were typically allocated four hectares of uncultivated land, but depending on land availability and the size of the ejido, they can request and usually work up to twenty hectares of land. In Kuchmil, *ejidatarios* cultivated on average three hectares, but a few *ejidatarios* cultivated up to twelve hectares of land.

19. Interview with Campos García, November 16, 2000. See also Kray 2006.

20. Interview with Martínez, February 21, 2002.

21. Interview with Campos García, November 16, 2000.

22. I knew of one case where a family who lived in a house mortgaged through INFONAVIT was allowed to apply to INVIQROO for housing. The house was located a few blocks from the beach in an area recently devastated by a hurricane. The family made a persuasive claim that their ability to sell their home was compromised by its location, and they needed to move for safety reasons: the house was not sturdy enough to resist another

hurricane. INVIQROO processed their application, but they had not yet received a parcel of land in 2001.

23. Interview with Campos García, November 16, 2000.

24. This political involvement is not new. Maya women are active participants in local politics in Kuchmil. Both single and married women often attend political rallies and meetings, in many instances without their husbands in the case of those who are married. In Kuchmil, politics cannot be divorced from issues of land and work because access to land is automatically linked with political participation; membership in the ejido designates male participants with the right to vote on all local issues and government policies that affect agricultural production. While women are not given an official vote, they actively participate in debating these issues during public forums and privately discuss these issues with their husbands and fathers. Alternatively, women can hold public office as health *promotoras* (promoters) and managers of the corn mill. Consequently, political engagement and activism forms a significant part of membership in an ejido community and Maya society. For further discussion, see Castellanos 2010b.

25. Personal communication with Alejandro Handall Díaz, financial advisor and interim director of INFOVIR, May 23, 2006.

26. See "Vivienda" [Housing], Government of Quintana Roo, n.d., accessed March 1, 2019, https://qroo.gob.mx/eje-5-crecimiento-ordenado-con-sustentabilidad-ambiental /vivienda.

Chapter Two

1. The construction of Paseos Kabah included several phases. In the first phase, one-bedroom units sized at 52 square meters were built on lots of 80 square meters. Plot sizes for social housing typically range from 60 to 140 square meters (Bredenoord and Cabrera Montiel 2014). Georgia Hartman (forthcoming) points out that construction was not intended to survive longer than fifty years.

2. These funds can now also be used to build a home, remodel one, or repay an existing mortgage.

3. Vicente Fox's speech at the ceremony to present FOVISSSTE's cofinancing program and to hand out housing titles. Electronic document, accessed November 15, 2007, http:// www.sadasi.com/testimoniales/news21.htm.

4. Fox's efforts are also rooted in past US efforts to use American homeownership as tool for development globally by normalizing consumption and expanding the middle class (Kwak 2015).

5. Statistic from http://www.sedatu.gob.mx/sraweb/noticias/noticias-2012/junio-2012 /12318/ (accessed March 11, 2014).

6. Interview with Fox, *Commanding Heights*.

7. "The War between Banks and 'Sofoles' Propels Mexican Real Estate," Wharton University of Pennsylvania, February 8, 2006, https://knowledge.wharton.upenn.edu/article/the -war-between-banks-and-sofoles-propels-mexican-real-estate/.

8. The statistics on housing were provided by Sebastián Fernández Cortina, "Housing in Practice" Roundtable, "Housing Across Borders: Mexico and U.S. Housing in Perspective"

Symposium, Center for U.S.-Mexican Studies, UC San Diego School of Global Policy and Strategy, May 26, 2017.

9. Drucilla Barker presented these ideas at the Crisis Economics Conference held on November 14, 2013, at the Institute for Advanced Study, University of Minnesota. These sentiments are most clearly articulated in *Liberating Economics* (Barker, Bergeron, and Feiner, forthcoming).

10. See http://www.sadasi.com/testimoniales/news21.htm (accessed November 15, 2007).

11. For an overview of Mexico's housing policies over the past five decades, see Bredenoord and Cabrera Montiel 2014.

12. This idea of individual property ownership dates back to Mexican independence from Spain. Mexican liberals considered "the individual property owner, freed from corporate restrictions on the pursuit of self-interest," as the person "who would provide the basis for political peace and economic prosperity in nineteenth-century Mexico" (Purnell 1999, 88).

13. For an overview of how INFONAVIT's policies have shifted over time, see Hartman 2017.

14. "War between Banks." See also Herbert, Belsky, and DuBroff 2012.

15. See the International Finance Corporation website, http://www.ifc.org.

16. Vicente Fox's February 2006 speech at the ceremony to present FOVISSSTE's cofinancing program and to hand out housing titles, http://www.sadasi.com/testimoniales /news21.htm (accessed November 15, 2007).

17. "Immigrants in U.S. Buy Mexico Homes with Cross-Border Loans," *Mercury News* (San Jose, CA), March 7, 2008, https://www.mercurynews.com/2008/03/07/immigrants-in -u-s-buy-mexico-homes-with-cross-border-loans/.

18. See http://www.sucasita.com.mx (accessed November 15, 2007).

19. Barker presented these words at the Crisis Economics Conference, November 14, 2013. See also Barker et al. Forthcoming.

20. See https://www.gob.mx/epn/prensa/infonavit-is-the-main-mexican-state-institution -for-ensuring-that-families-can-exercise-their-constitutional-right-to-decent-housing-epn (accessed November 19, 2016).

21. Interview with Ing. Ramón López Gual, Grupo Sadasi, December 13, 2011.

22. See the CADU Inmobiliaria profile, 2019, accessed April 29, 2020, http://ri .caduinmobiliaria.com/en/perfil.

Chapter Three

1. "Is NAFTA Good for Farmers?" CBS News, July 1, 2006, https://www.cbsnews.com /news/is-nafta-good-for-mexicos-farmers/.

2. For a discussion of the shrinking of the middle class, see L. Walker 2013.

3. "President Vicente Fox Invited the Managing Director of Bangladesh's Grameen Bank to Lunch," Press Release, Office of the President, July 17, 2003, http://fox.presidencia.gob .mx/en/activities/pressreleases/?contenido=5819&pagina=14.

4. Ninety-seven percent of Grameen's clients are women. See "Introduction," Grameen Bank website, December 2019, http://www.grameen.com/introduction/.

5. Interview with Fox, *Commanding Heights*.

6. Jim Boulden, "The Birth of Microcredit," CNN.com Europe, March 29, 2001, http://edition.cnn.com/BUSINESS/programs/yourbusiness/stories2001/lending/.

7. Interview with Fox, *Commanding Heights*.

8. See Cohen 2003.

9. The total annual cost (Costo Anual Total or CAT) was 106.5 percent before taxes. See "Crédito mujer," Compartamos Banco website, n.d., accessed May 13, 2020, https://www.compartamos.com.mx/compartamos/credito/credito-grupal. The high interest rates for microfinance loans are attributed to greed, high operational costs, or loss due to loan defaults. See Macchiavello 2018 and "Why are microcredit interest rates higher than traditional interest rates?" Microworld website, accessed June 8, 2020, https://www.microworld.org/en/news-from-the-field/article/why-are-microcredit-interest-rates-higher-traditional-interest-rates. In comparison to other countries, microfinance interest rates in Mexico are on the high end. See Macchiavello 2018 and "Variations in Microcredit Interest Rates," CGAP website, accessed June 8, 2020, https://www.cgap.org/sites/default/files/CGAP-Brief-Are-Microcredit-Interest-Rates-Excessive-Feb-2009.pdf.

10. Manuela Angelucci, Dean Karlan, and Jonathan Zinman, "Microcredit for Women in Mexico," Innovations for Poverty Action, n.d., accessed October 4, 2018, https://www.poverty-action.org/study/microcredit-women-mexico.

11. See https://www.womensworldbanking.org/about-us/partnerships/network-associates/compartamos-banco/ (accessed September 26, 2018).

12. Angelucci et al., "Microcredit."

13. See https://www.sadasi.com/desarrollos-sadasi/desarrollos-en-quintana-roo/cancun/prado-norte/ (accessed March 20, 2019).

14. Erin Carlyle, "Mexico's Credit Card." *Forbes*, April 25, 2012, https://www.forbes.com/global/2012/0507/global-2000-12-grupo-elektra-ricardo-salinas-pliego-mexico-credit-card.html#56793f73203b.

15. Carlyle, "Mexico's Credit Card."

16. See "Is a Credit Card Debt Crisis Looming in Mexico?" Banderas News, September 2007, accessed March 20, 2019, http://banderasnews.com/0709/edat-creditcardcrisis.htm.

17. Aaron Childree, "Improving Credit Access in Mexico," Borgen Project, December 14, 2017, https://borgenproject.org/improving-credit-access-in-mexico/.

18. See "Overview: National Financial Inclusion Strategies," World Bank, November 11, 2015, accessed March 26, 2019, http://www.worldbank.org/en/topic/financialinclusion/brief/national-financial-inclusion-strategies.

19. Childree, "Improving Credit Access."

20. See "MX: Expanding Rural Finance," World Bank, accessed March 26, 2019, http://projects.worldbank.org/P153338?lang=en.

21. See "Mexico to Accelerate Path to Financial Inclusion," World Bank, June 23, 2016, http://www.worldbank.org/en/news/feature/2016/06/23/mexico-to-accelerate-path-to-financial-inclusion.

22. Stefanie Eschenbacher, "Mexico's New Government Wants Fintech, Banks to Help with Financial Inclusion," Reuters World News, August 21, 2018, https://www.reuters.com

/article/us-mexico-politics/mexicos-new-government-wants-fintech-banks-to-help-financial
-inclusion-idUSKCN1L704E.

Chapter Four

1. Guillermo Trejo (2012) documents that while Indigenous collective action increased dramatically in response to neoliberal reforms and state repression, this cycle of revolt declined with the rise of leftist parties and fair elections.

2. See Kasey Keeler (2016) for a discussion of American Indians and housing in the United States. For a discussion of housing policies among aboriginals in Canada, see A. Anderson 2013. For a comparative analysis of housing policies and race in the United States and Canada, see Hugill 2019.

3. This price is based on the price of the dollar in 2005, when the house was purchased.

4. For a historical overview of the UDI system, see Lipscomb, Harvey, and Hunt 2003.

5. To jumpstart its economy during the Franco dictatorship, Spain had turned toward property ownership; by the 1980s, the economy was dependent on tourism, property development, and construction (López and Rodríguez 2011). This dependency deepened through the crisis that plagued the country during the 1990s and the following decade. As a result, Spain was especially vulnerable when the global housing bubble burst.

6. Peter Krupa, "Time Running Out for Su Casita." BN Americas, September 21, 2010, https://www.bnamericas.com/en/news/banking/FEATURE:_Time_running_out_for_Su _Casita/.

7. Peter Krupa, "Su Casita Seeking to Avoid Bankruptcy with Debt Restructuring Talks," BN Americas, September 30, 2010, https://www.bnamericas.com/en/news/Su_Casita_seeking _to_avoid_bankruptcy_with_debt_restructuring_talks.

8. "Evaluación de Administrador de Activos: Tertius S.A.P.I. de C.V. SOFOM, E.N.R.," Standard and Poor's Ratings Services, December 4, 2014, https://www.standardandpoors.com /es_LA/delegate/getPDF?articleId=1578101&type=COMMENTS&subType=.

9. Richard Marosi, "A Subprime Horror," *Los Angeles Times*, November 26, 2017, http:// www.latimes.com/projects/la-me-mexico-housing-chapter-4/.

10. Marosi, "Subprime Horror."

11. Marosi.

12. Interview with INFONAVIT representative, January 14, 2015.

13. See the special issue on "Race, Empire, and the Crisis of the Subprime" of the *American Quarterly*, especially Chakravarty and Ferreira da Silva 2012. Also, see Moten 2013.

14. See Marosi, "Subprime Horror"; Inclán-Valadez 2013; Fuentes and Hernandez 2014; Monkkonen 2014.

15. Interview with INFONAVIT representative, January 15, 2015.

16. Interview with INFONAVIT, January 15, 2015.

17. See "Race, Empire, and the Crisis of the Subprime," *American Quarterly* 64 (3).

18. Interview with CONDUSEF representative Juan Bosco García Galán, January 22, 2015.

19. Interview with Tertius representative, February 16, 2015.

20. Interview with Tertius representative, February 16, 2015.

21. Interview with Tertius representative, February 16, 2015.

22. Interview with INFONAVIT representative, January 14, 2015.

23. Interview with Tertius representative, February 16, 2015.

24. Sebastián Fernández Cortina, "Housing in Practice" roundtable, "Housing across Borders: Mexico and US Housing in Perspective" symposium, Center for U.S.-Mexico Studies, University of California San Diego School of Global Policy and Strategy, May 26, 2017.

25. See OECD 2015; Organisation for Economic Co-operation and Development Affordable Housing Database, *http://www.oecd.org/social/affordable-housing-database.htm*.

26. According to Paul Sullivan, Mayas take "the past to be the harbinger of future times and events" (1989, xvi). Prophecy is central to Maya thought, culture, and language.

Chapter Five

1. Undeveloped land within Cancún's urban planning zone is scarce. Migrants who opt to squat do so in colonias newly established outside the city's urban boundaries. Jonathan Salazar Santos, Observatorio Urbano Local, Cancún, pers. comm., January 8, 2015.

2. Although Cancún provides a wide variety of quality public and private schools and medical facilities, it is very difficult for migrants to access these resources.

3. In 2010, journalist Roberto Lovato dubbed Cancún the "suicide capital" of Mexico. See Lovato 2010. Although Cancún continues to suffer high suicide rates, especially among adolescents, it was surpassed by Chihuahua, Moroleón-Uniangato, Mérida, San Francisco del Rincón, and Celaya in 2015. See "Voluntary National Review for the High-Level Political Forum on Sustainable Development," Federal Government, Mexico, 2018, https://www.gob.mx/cms/uploads/attachment/file/345549/VOLUNTARY_NATIONAL_REPORT.pdf. For a study of the impact of violence on youth in Cancún, see Perla Orquídea Fragoso Lugo 2016.

4. For an overview of Antorcha Campesina's history, see the description on their website at www.antorchacampesina.org.mx/quienessomos.php.

5. Interview with Antorcha representative David Sánchez Reyes, January 24, 2015.

Epilogue

1. Marc Filippino, "Levittown and the Rise of the American Suburb," Public Radio International, December 4, 2017, https://www.pri.org/stories/2017-12-04/levittown-and-rise-american-suburb.

2. Marosi, "Subprime Horror." Also see Luis Triveno, "How Latin America's Housing Policies Are Changing the Lives of Urban Families," World Bank blog, April 11, 2016, https://blogs.worldbank.org/sustainablecities/how-latin-america-s-housing-policies-are-changing-lives-urban-families.

3. We can see this at work in the segregation of America's cities. Racial covenants prevented African American families from purchasing homes in suburbs like Levittown, while gentrification is increasingly pricing working-class families and minorities out of the city. For a discussion of racial covenants in American cities, see C. Anderson 2017, Goetz 2018,

Gotham 2014, Michney 2017, and Satter 2010. Also see Ta-Nehisi Coates, "The Case for Reparations," *The Atlantic*, June 19, 2014, https://www.theatlantic.com/magazine/archive/2014/06/the-case-for-reparations/361631/.

4. See "No habrá desalojos por adeudos de Infonavit: López Obrador," *Excelsior*, February 19, 2020, https://www.excelsior.com.mx/nacional/no-habra-desalojos-por-adeudos-al-infonavit-lopez-obrador/1364989; Helgi Godmundsson, "AMLO Urges Infonavit to Restructure Loans, End Foreclosures," S&P Global Market Intelligence, June 19, 2019, https://www.spglobal.com/marketintelligence/en/news-insights/trending/bXmQJ2IrB2TeSbwiKM3IOw2.

5. See Lizzie Presser, "Kicked off the Land: Why So Many Black Families Are Losing Their Property." *New Yorker*, July 15, 2019, https://www.newyorker.com/magazine/2019/07/22/kicked-off-the-land.

References

Abrams, Philip. 1988. "Notes on the Difficulty of Studying the State." *Journal of Historical Sociology* 1 (1): 58–79.

Ahmed, Sarah, Claudia Castañeda, Anne-Marie Fortier, and Mimi Sheller, eds. 2003. *Uprootings/Regroundings: Questions of Home and Migration*. Oxford, UK: Berg.

Aikau, Hokulani K. and Vernadette Vicuña Gonzalez, eds. 2019. *Detours: A Decolonial Guide to Hawai'i*. Durham, NC: Duke University Press.

Altamirano-Jiménez, Isabel. 2017. "The State Is Not a Savior: Indigenous Law, Gender and the Neoliberal State in Oaxaca." In *Making Sense of Indigenous Feminism*, edited by Joyce Green, 215–33. Winnipeg, MB, Canada: Fernwood.

Anderson, Alan B., ed. 2013. *Home in the City: Urban Aboriginal Housing and Living Conditions*. Toronto: University of Toronto Press.

Anderson, Carol. 2017. *White Rage: The Unspoken Truth of Our Racial Divide*. New York: Bloomsbury.

Arvin, Maile, Eve Tuck, and Angie Morrill. 2013. "Decolonizing Feminism: Challenging Connections between Settler Colonialism and Heteropatriarchy." *Feminist Formations* 25(1): 8–34.

Assies, Willem. 2008. "Land Tenure and Tenure Regimes in Mexico: An Overview." *Journal of Agrarian Change* 8 (1): 33–63.

Auerbach, Nancy. 2018. *States, Banks, and Markets Mexico's Path to Financial Liberalization in Comparative Perspective*. Boulder, CO: Westview.

Auyero, Javier. 2012. *Patients of the State: The Politics of Waiting in Argentina*. Durham, NC: Duke University Press.

Babb, Florence E. 2001. *After Revolution: Mapping Gender and Cultural Politics in Neoliberal Nicaragua*. Austin: University of Texas Press.

———. 2011. *The Tourism Encounter: Fashioning Latin American Nations and Histories*. Stanford, CA: Stanford University Press.

Baldy, Cutcha Risling. 2018. *We Are Dancing for You: Native Feminisms and the Revitalization of Women's Coming-of-Age Ceremonies.* Seattle: University of Washington Press.

Baitenmann, Helga. 1997. "Rural Agency and State Formation in Post-Revolutionary Mexico: The Agrarian Reform in Central Veracruz (1915–1992)." PhD diss., New School for Social Research, New York.

————. 1998. "The Article 27 Reforms and the Promise of Local Democratization in Central Veracruz." In *The Transformation of Rural Mexico: Reforming the Ejido Sector*, edited by Wayne A. Cornelius and David Myhre, 105–23. La Jolla, CA: Center for U.S.-Mexican Studies.

————. 2005. "Counting on State Subjects: State Formation and Citizenship in Twentieth-Century Mexico." In *State Formation: Anthropological Perspectives*, edited by Christian Krohn-Hansen and Knut G. Nustad, 171–94. London: Pluto Press.

Barker, Drucilla K., Suzanne Bergeron, and Susan F. Feiner. Forthcoming. *Liberating Economics: Feminist Perspectives on Families, Work, and Globalization.* Ann Arbor: University of Michigan Press.

Barker, Drucilla K., and Susan F. Feiner. 2004. *Liberating Economics: Feminist Perspectives on Families, Work, and Globalization.* Ann Arbor: University of Michigan Press.

Barker, Joanne. 2017. Introduction to *Critically Sovereign: Indigenous, Gender, Sexuality, and Feminist Studies*, 1–45. Edited by Joanne Barker. Durham, NC: Duke University Press.

Barnes, Grenville. 2009. "The Evolution and Resilience of Community-Based Land Tenure in Rural Mexico." *JLUP Land Use Policy* 26 (2): 393–400.

Bayat, Asef. 2000. "From 'Dangerous Classes' to 'Quiet Rebels': Politics of the Urban Subaltern in the Global South." *International Sociology* 15 (3): 533–57.

————. 2010. *Life as Politics: How Ordinary People Change the Middle East.* Amsterdam: Amsterdam University Press.

Beck, Ulrich. 2008. *World at Risk.* Cambridge, UK: Polity Press.

Bergdoll, Barry, Carlos Eduardo Comas, Jorge Francisco Liernur, and Patricio de Real, eds. 2015. *Latin American in Construction: Architecture 1955–1980.* New York: The Museum of Modern Art.

Bonfil Batalla, Guillermo. 1996. *México Profundo: Reclaiming a Civilization.* Translated by Philip A. Denis. Austin: University of Texas Press.

Botey, Carlota. 1998. "Mujer rural: reforma agraria y contrarreforma." In *Tiempo de crisis, tiempo de mujeres*, edited by Josefina Aranda, Carlota Botey, and Rosario Robles, 95–154. Oaxaca: Universidad Autónoma Benito Juárez de Oaxaca (UABJO), Centro de Estudios de la Cuestión Agraria Mexicana A.C.

Bourdieu, Pierre. 2005. *The Social Structures of the Economy.* Cambridge, UK: Polity Press.

Brannon, Jeffrey T. 1991. "Conclusion: Yucatecan Political Economy in Broader Perspective." In *Land, Labor, and Capital in Modern Yucatán: Essays in Regional History and Political Economy*, edited by Jeffrey T. Brannon and Gilbert M. Joseph, 243–49. Tuscaloosa: University of Alabama Press.

Bredenoord, Jan, and Lorena Cabrera Montiel. 2014. "Affordable Housing for Low-Income Groups in Mexico and Urban Housing Challenges of Today." In *Affordable Housing in the Urban Global South: Seeking Sustainable Solutions,* edited by Jan Bredenoord, Paul van Lindert, and Peter Smets, 221–40. London: Routledge.

Bredenoord, Jan, Paul van Lindert, and Peter Smets, eds. 2014. *Affordable Housing in the Urban Global South: Seeking Sustainable Solutions.* London: Routledge.

Bruhn, Miriam and Inessa Love. 2014. "The Real Impact of Improved Access to Finance: Evidence from Mexico." *Journal of Finance* 69 (3): 1347–76.

Byrd, Jodi A. 2011. *The Transit of Empire: Indigenous Critiques of Colonialism.* Minneapolis: University of Minnesota Press.

Caldeira, Teresa. 2001. *City of Walls. Crime, Segregation, and Citizenship in São Paulo.* Berkeley: University of California Press.

Canessa, Andrew. 2012. *Intimate Indigeneities: Race, Sex, and History in the Small Spaces of Andean Life.* Durham, NC: Duke University Press.

Carpio, Myla Vicenti. 2011. *Indigenous Albuquerque.* Lubbock: Texas Tech University Press.

Carsten, Janet. 2004. *After Kinship.* Cambridge: Cambridge University Press.

Carsten, Janet, and Stephen Hugh-Jones, eds. 1995. *About the House: Lévi-Strauss and Beyond.* Cambridge: Cambridge University Press.

Castellanos, M. Bianet. 2010a. *A Return to Servitude: Maya Migration and the Tourist Trade in Cancún.* Minneapolis: University of Minnesota Press.

———. 2010b. "Don Teo's Expulsion: Property Regimes, Moral Economies, and Ejido Reform." *Journal of Latin American and Caribbean Anthropology* 15 (1): 144–69.

———. 2017. "Introduction: Settler Colonialism in Latin America." *American Quarterly* 69 (4): 777–81.

———, ed. 2019. *Detours: Travel and the Ethics of Research in the Global South.* Tucson: University of Arizona Press.

Castellanos, M. Bianet, and Matilde Córdoba Azcárate. Forthcoming. "Guardians of Tradition: The Popular Geopolitics of Yucatec Maya Women on Tour." In *The Geopolitics of Tourism: Assemblages of Power, Mobility and the State,* edited by Mary Mostafanezhad, Matilde Córdoba Azcárate, and Roger Norum. Tucson: University of Arizona Press.

Castro, Juan, and Manuela Lavinas Picq. 2017. "Stateness as Land Grab: A Political History of Maya Dispossession in Guatemala." *American Quarterly* 69 (4): 791–99.

Cattelino, Jessica R. 2008. *High Stakes Florida Seminole Gaming and Sovereignty.* Durham, NC: Duke University Press.

Chakravarty, Paula, and Denise Ferreira de Silva. 2012. "Accumulation, Dispossession, and Debt: The Racial Logic of Capital Accumulation—An Introduction." *American Quarterly* 64 (3): 361–85.

Chang, David. A. 2010. *The Color of the Land: Race, Nation, and the Politics of Landownership in Oklahoma, 1832–1929.* Chapel Hill: University of North Carolina Press.

———. 2011. "Enclosures of Land and Sovereignty: The Allotment of American Indian Lands." *Radical History Review,* no. 109 (Winter): 108–19.

Chu, Julie Y. 2010. *Cosmologies of Credit: Transnational Mobility and the Politics of Destination in China.* Durham, NC: Duke University Press.

Clancy, Michael. 2001. *Exporting Paradise: Tourism and Development in Mexico.* New York: Pergamon.

Cohen, Lizbeth. 2003. *A Consumer's Republic: The Politics of Mass Consumption in Postwar America*. New York: Alfred A. Knopf.

Collier, George A. 1994. *Basta! Land and the Zapatista Rebellion in Chiapas*. Oakland, CA: First Food Books.

Con Uribe, María José. 2005. "The East Coast of Quintana Roo: A Brief Account of Archaeological Work." In *Quintana Roo Archaeology*, edited by Justine M. Shaw and Jennifer P. Matthews, 15–29. Tucson: University of Arizona Press.

Córdoba Azcárate, Matilde. 2020. *Stuck with Tourism: Space, Power, and Labor in Contemporary Yucatán*. Berkeley: University of California Press.

Córdoba Azcárate, Matilde, Idalina Baptista, and Fernando Domínguez Rubio. 2014. "Enclosures within Enclosures and Hurricane Reconstruction in Cancún, Mexico." *City & Society* 26 (1): 96–119. https://doi.org/10.1111/ciso.12026.

Cornelius, Wayne A. 1975. *Politics and the Migrant Poor in Mexico City*. Stanford, CA: Stanford University Press.

Cornelius, Wayne A., and David Myhre, eds. 1998. *The Transformation of Rural Mexico: Reforming the Ejido Sector*. La Jolla, CA: Center for U.S.-Mexican Studies.

Cortes, Rosalia. 2009. "Social Policy in Latin America in the Post-neoliberal Era." In *Governance after Neoliberalism in Latin America*, edited by Jean Grugel and Pía Riggirozzi, 49–65. New York: Palgrave Macmillan.

Coulthard, Glen Sean. 2014. *Red Skin, White Masks: Rejecting the Colonial Politics of Recognition*. Minneapolis: University of Minnesota Press.

Crenshaw, Kimberle. 1991. "Mapping the Margins: Intersectionality, Identity Politics, and Violence against Women of Color." *Stanford Law Review* 43 (6): 1241–99.

Cronon, William. 1983. *Changes in the Land: Indians, Colonists, and the Ecology of New England*. New York: Hill and Wang.

Dachary, Alfredo César. 1998. *El Caribe Mexicano: una frontera olvidada*. Chetumal: Universidad de Quintana Roo; Fundación de Parques y Museos de Cozumel.

Daniel, Peter. 2015. *Dispossession: Discrimination against African American Farmers in the Age of Civil Rights*. Chapel Hill: University of North Carolina Press.

Dávila, Arlene. 2012. *Culture Works: Space, Value, and Mobility across the Neoliberal Americas*. New York: New York University Press.

Davis, Diane Emily. 1994. *Urban Leviathan: Mexico City in the Twentieth Century*. Philadelphia: Temple University Press.

———. 2016. *Building Better Cities with Strategic Investments in Social Housing*, vol. 1, December 2016. https://research.gsd.harvard.edu/socialhousingmexico/files/2014/10/BetterCities_FINAL_121616.pdf.

Davis, Diane Emily and Nora Ruth Libertun de Duren, eds. 2011. *Cities & Sovereignty: Identity Politics in Urban Spaces*. Bloomington: Indiana University Press.

Davis, Mike. 2006. *Planet of Slums*. London: Verso.

De Noriega Olea, Federico, Maria Aldonza Sakar Almirante and Carlos Eduardo Romero Sotelo. 2019. "Mexico." In *The Consumer Finance Law Review*, edited by Rick Fischer, Obrea Poindexter and Jeremy Mandel, 111-25. London: Law Business Research.

De Soto, Hernando. 1989. *The Other Path: The Economic Answer to Terrorism*. New York: Basic Books.

———. 2000. *The Mystery of Capital: Why Capitalism Triumphs in the West and Fails Everywhere Else*. New York: Basic Books.

Deere, Carmen Diana, and Magdalena León de Leal. 2001. *Empowering Women: Land and Property Rights in Latin America*. Pittsburgh: University of Pittsburgh Press.

———. 2002. "Individual versus Collective Land Rights: Tensions between Women's and Indigenous Rights under Neoliberalism." In *The Spaces of Neoliberalism: Land, Place and Family in Latin America*, edited by Jacquelyn Chase, 53–86. Bloomfield, CT: Kumarian Press.

Desmond, Matthew. 2016. *Evicted: Poverty and Profit in the American City*. New York: Crown.

Di Giminiani, Piergiorgio. 2018. *Sentient Lands: Indigeneity, Property, and Political Imagination in Neoliberal Chile*. Tucson: University of Arizona Press.

Dinzey-Flores, Zaire Z. 2013. *Locked in, Locked out: Gated Communities in a Puerto Rican City*. Philadelphia: University of Pennsylvania Press.

Dorries, Heather, Robert Henry, David Hugill, Tyler McCreary, and Juli Tomiak, eds. 2019. *Settler City Limits: Indigenous Resurgence and Colonial Violence in the Urban Prairie West*. East Lansing: Michigan State University Press.

Douglas, Mary, and Aaron Wildavsky. 1983. *Risk and Culture: An Essay on the Selection of Technical and Environmental Dangers*. Berkeley: University of California Press.

Eckstein, Susan Eva. 1977. *The Poverty of Revolution: The State and the Urban Poor in Mexico*. Princeton, NJ: Princeton University Press.

Eisenstadt, Todd. 2011. *Politics, Identity, and Mexico's Indigenous Rights Movements*. Cambridge: Cambridge University Press.

Eiss, Paul K. 2002. "Redemption's Archive: Remembering the Future in a Revolutionary Past." *Comparative Studies in Society and History : An International Quarterly* 44 (1): 106–36.

———. 2010. *In the Name of El Pueblo: Place, Community, and the Politics of History in Yucatán*. Durham, NC: Duke University Press.

Elias, Christopher, and Travis Ritchie. 2008. *Housing Microfinance in Latin America: Opportunities in Mexico*. APP Report. Los Angeles: UCLA School of Public Affairs.

Ellis, Edward A., Karen A. Kainer, José Antonio Sierra Huelsz, Patricia Negreros-Castillo, and Maria DiGiano. 2014. "Community-Based Forest Management in Quintana Roo, Mexico." In *Forests under Pressure: Local Responses to Global Issues*, edited by Pia Katila, Glenn Galloway, Wil de Jong, Pablo Pacheco, and Gerardo Mery, 131–51. Mexico City: International Union of Forest Research Organization (IUFRO).

Ellison, Susan Helen. 2018. *Domesticating Democracy: The Politics of Conflict Resolution in Bolivia*. Durham, NC: Duke University Press.

Elyachar, Julia. 2002. "Empowerment Money: The World Bank, Non-Governmental Organizations, and the Value of Culture in Egypt." *Public Culture* 14 (3): 493–513.

Encuesta Intercensal. 2015. "Panorama sociodemográfico de Quintana Roo 2015." Mexico City: Instituto Nacional de Estadística y Geografía.

Encuesta Nacional de Inclusión Financiera (ENIF). 2015. *México, inclusión financiera: principales hallazgos.* Mexico City: INEGI, CNBV.

Escobar, Arturo. 1995. *Encountering Development: The Making and Unmaking of the Third World.* Princeton, NJ: Princeton University Press.

———. 2018. *Designs for the Pluriverse: Radical Interdependence, Autonomy, and the Making of Worlds.* Durham, NC: Duke University Press.

Farriss, Nancy M. 1984. *Maya Society under Colonial Rule: The Collective Enterprise of Survival.* Princeton, NJ: Princeton University Press.

Federal Government, Mexico. 2018. "Voluntary National Review for the High-Level Political Forum on Sustainable Development: Basis for a Long-Term Sustainable Development Vision in Mexico." https://www.gob.mx/cms/uploads/attachment/file/345549/VOLUNTARY_NATIONAL_REPORT.pdf.

Ferry, Elizabeth. 2002. "Inalienable Commodities: The Production and Circulation of Silver and Patrimony in a Mexican Mining Cooperative." *Cultural Anthropology: Journal of the Society for Cultural Anthropology* 17 (3): 331–58.

Fischer, Brodwyn. 2014. Introduction to *Cities from Scratch: Poverty and Informality in Urban Latin America*, edited by Brodwyn Fischer, Bryan McCann, and Javier Auyero, 1–7. Durham, NC: Duke University Press.

Fischer, Brodwyn, Bryan McCann, and Javier Auyero, eds. 2014. *Cities from Scratch: Poverty and Informality in Urban Latin America.* Durham, NC: Duke University Press.

Fixico, Donald L. 2000. *The Urban Indian Experience in America.* Albuquerque: University of New Mexico Press.

Forbes, Jack. 2001. "The Urban Tradition among Native Americans." In *American Indians and the Urban Experience,* edited by Susan Lobo and Kurt Peters, 5–25. Walnut Creek, CA: Altamira Press.

Forrest, Ray and Ngai-Ming Yip, eds. 2013. *Young People and Housing: Transitions, Trajectories and Generational Fractures.* New York: Routledge.

Fragoso Lugo, Perla Orquídea. 2016. *A puro golpe: Violencias y malestares sociales en la juventud cancunense.* Tuxtla Gutiérrez, Mexico: Universidad de Ciencias y Artes de Chiapas.

Fraser, Valerie. 2001. *Building the New World: Modern Architecture in Latin America 1930–1960.* New York: Verso.

Fuentes, César M, and Vladimir Hernandez. 2014. "Housing Finance Reform in Mexico: The Impact of Housing Vacancy on Property Crime." *International Journal of Housing Policy* 14 (4): 368–88.

García de Fuentes, Ana. 1979. *Cancún: Turismo y Subdesarrollo Regional.* México: Universidad Nacional Autonóma de México (UNAM).

Gilbert, Alan. 1993. *In Search of a Home: Rental and Shared Housing in Latin America.* London: UCL Press.

Gilbert, Alan, and Ann Varley. 1991. *Landlord and Tenant: Housing the Poor in Urban Mexico.* London: Routledge.

Gilbert, Alan, and Peter M. Ward. 1985. *Housing, the State, and the Poor: Policy and Practice in Three Latin American Cities.* Cambridge: Cambridge University Press.

Gilbert, Dennis L. 2007. *Mexico's Middle Class in the Neoliberal Era*. Tucson: University of Arizona Press.

Gledhill, John. 1995. *Neoliberalism, Transnationalization, and Rural Poverty: A Case Study of Michoacán, Mexico*. Boulder, CO: Westview.

Goeman, Mishuana R. 2017. "Ongoing Storms and Struggles: Gendered Violence and Resource Exploitation." In *Critically Sovereign: Indigenous Gender, Sexuality, and Feminist Studies*, edited by Joanne Barker, 99–126. Durham, NC: Duke University Press.

Goetz, Edward G. 2018. *The One-Way Street of Integration: Fair Housing and the Pursuit of Racial Justice in American Cities*. Ithaca, NY: Cornell University Press.

Goldstein, Daniel M. 2004. *Outlawed: Between Security and Rights in a Bolivian City*. Durham, NC: Duke University Press.

González Montes, Soledad. 1988. "La reproducción de la desigualdad entre los sexos: Prácticas e ideología de la herencia en una comunidad campesina (Xalatlaco, Estado de México, 1920–1960)." In *Las mujeres en el campo*, edited by Josefina Aranda Bezaury, 65–81. Oaxaca: UABJO.

Goodale, Mark, and Nancy Grey Postero, eds. 2013. *Neoliberalism, Interrupted: Social Change and Contested Governance in Contemporary Latin America*. Stanford, CA: Stanford University Press.

Gotham, Kevin Fox. 2002. *Race, Real Estate, and Uneven Development: The Kansas City Experience, 1900–2000*. Albany: State University of New York Press.

Gott, Richard. 2007. "Latin America as White Settler Society." *Bulletin of Latin American Research* 26 (2): 269–89.

Graeber, David. 2012. *Debt: The First 5,000 Years*. Brooklyn, NY: Melville House.

Grammont, Hubert C. de. 2001. *El Barzón: clase media, ciudadanía y democracia*. Mexico: Instituto de Investigaciones Sociales, Editorial Plaza y Valdés Editores.

Green, Joyce, ed. 2017. *Making Space for Indigenous Feminism*. Winnipeg, MB, Canada: Fernwood.

Grugel, Jean, and Pía Riggirozzi, eds. 2009. *Governance after Neoliberalism in Latin America*. New York: Palgrave Macmillan.

Gupta, Akhil. 1995. "Blurred Boundaries: The Discourse of Corruption, the Culture of Politics, and the Imagined State." *American Ethnologist* 22 (2): 375–402.

———. 2012. *Red Tape: Bureaucracy, Structural Violence, and Poverty in India*. Durham, NC: Duke University Press.

Guseva, Alya. 2008. *Into the Red: The Birth of the Credit Card Market in Postcommunist Russia*. Stanford, CA: Stanford University Press.

Gutiérrez Nájera, Lourdes, and Korinta Maldonado. 2017. "Transnational Settler Colonial Formations and Global Capital: A Consideration of Indigenous Mexican Migrants." *American Quarterly* 69 (4): 809–21.

Guyer, Jane I. 2004. *Marginal Gains: Monetary Transactions in Atlantic Africa*. Chicago: The University of Chicago Press.

Haber, Stephen. 2005. "Mexico's Experiments with Bank Privatization and Liberalization, 1991–2003." *Journal of Banking and Finance* 29: 2325–53.

Hale, Charles. 2006. *Más Que Un Indio: Racial Ambivalence and Neoliberal Multiculturalism in Guatemala*. Santa Fe, NM: School of American Research Press.

Han, Clara. 2012. *Life in Debt: Times of Care and Violence in Neoliberal Chile*. Berkeley:
University of California Press.

Hansson, Anna Granath, and Björn Lundgren. 2019. "Defining Social Housing: A Discussion on the Suitable Criteria." *Housing, Theory and Society* 36 (2): 149–66. DOI:
10.1080/14036096.2018.1459826.

Harjo, Laura. 2019. *Spiral to the Stars: Mvskoke Tools of Futurity*. Tucson: University of
Arizona Press.

Hartman, Georgia. 2017. "'To Have Something for My Children': Patrimonio and Mortgage Finance in Mexico." In *Mortgage across Cultures: Land, Finance, and Epistemology*,
edited by Daivi Rodima-Taylor and Parker Shipton, 61–69. Boston: Land Mortgage
Working Group Research Report.

———. Forthcoming. "'Homes with Value': Mortgage Finance, Patrimony, and the
Incommensurability of Home Value in Urban Mexico." *City & Society*.

Harvey, David. 2004. "The 'New' Imperialism: Accumulation by Dispossession." *The
Socialist Register* 40: 63–87.

———. 2005. *A Brief History of Neoliberalism*. Oxford: Oxford University Press.

———. 2011. "The Future of the Commons." *Radical History Review* 2011 (109): 101–7.

Hellman, Judith Adler. 1995. *Mexican Lives*. New York: New Press.

Herbert, Christopher E., Eric Belsky, and Nicholas DuBroff. 2012. "The State of Mexico's
Housing—Recent Progress and Continued Challenges." Working paper. Mexico City:
Fundación Centro de Investigaciones y Documentación de la Casa A.C. (CIDOC).

Herrera, Veronica. 2017. *Water and Politics: Clientilism and Reform in Urban Mexico*. Ann
Arbor: University of Michigan Press.

Herzog, Tamar. 2013. "Colonial Law and 'Native Customs': Indigenous Land Rights in
Colonial Spanish America." *The Americas* 69 (3): 303–21.

Ho, Karen. 2009. *Liquidated: An Ethnography of Wall Street*. Durham, NC: Duke University Press.

Holston, James. 1989. *The Modernist City: An Anthropological Critique of Brasilia*. Chicago:
University of Chicago Press.

———. 2008. *Insurgent Citizenship: Disjunctions of Democracy and Modernity in Brazil*.
Princeton, NJ: Princeton University Press.

Holston, James, and Arjun Appadurai. 1999. Introduction to *Cities and Citizenship*, edited
by James Holston, 2–18. Durham, NC: Duke University Press.

Horn, Philipp. 2019. *Indigenous Rights to the City: Ethnicity and Urban Planning in Bolivia
and Ecuador*. London: Routledge.

"Housing in Mexico: An Overlooked Revolution." 2004 (August 26). *The Economist*.
http://www.economist.com/World/la/PrinterFriendly.cfm?Story_ID=3131672.

Hugill, David. 2019. "Comparative Settler Colonial Urbanisms: Racism and the Making
of Inner-City Winnipeg and Minneapolis, 1940–1975." In *Settler City Limits: Indigenous Resurgence and Colonial Violence in the Urban Prairie West*, edited by Heather

Dorries, Robert Henry, David Hugill, Tyler McCreary, and Juli Tomiak, 70–91. East Lansing: Michigan State University Press.

Immigration and Refugee Board of Canada. 2008. *Mexico: Treatment of Indigenous People in Urban Areas; State Protection Efforts (2005-2007)*, January 17, 2008, https://www.refworld.org/docid/47ce6d7f32.html.

Inclán-Valadez, María Cristina. 2013. "The 'Casas Geo' Movement: An Ethnography of a New Housing Experience in Cuernavaca, Mexico." PhD dissertation, London School of Economics and Political Science, http://etheses.lse.ac.uk/726/.

———. 2014. "Building New Geographies in Urban Mexico: The Case of the Casas GEO." In *Transbordering Latin Americas: Liminal Places, Cultures, and Powers (T)Here*, edited by Clara Irazábal, 166–86. New York: Routledge.

INEGI (Instituto Nacional Estadístico, Geográfico e Informático). 2000. *Cuaderno estadístico municipal, edición 1999: Benito Juárez*. Estado de Quintana Roo, Mexico.

———. 2001. *XII Censo general de población y vivienda*. Mexico City.

International Finance Corporation (IFC). 2007. *Making a Difference: How Private Enterprise Is Creating Opportunity and Improving Lives in Developing Countries*. Washington, DC: World Bank.

Jackson, Shona N. 2012. *Creole Indigeneity: Between Myth and Nation in the Caribbean*. Minneapolis: University of Minnesota Press.

Jackson, Sue, Libby Porter, and Louise C. Johnson, eds. 2018. *Planning in Indigenous Australia: From Imperial Foundations to Postcolonial Futures*. London: Routledge.

James, Deborah. 2015. *Money from Nothing: Indebtedness and Aspiration in South Africa*. Stanford, CA: Stanford University Press.

Jha, Abhas K. 2007. "Low-Income Housing in Latin America and the Caribbean." En Breve, no. 101. Washington DC: World Bank. http://hdl.handle.net/10986/10301.

Joseph, Gilbert M. 1988. *Revolution from Without: Yucatán, Mexico, and the United States, 1880–1924*. Durham, NC: Duke University Press.

Joseph, Gilbert M. and Daniel Nugent, eds. 1994. *Everyday Forms of State Formation: Revolution and Negotiation of Rule in Modern Mexico*. Durham, NC: Duke University Press.

Joseph, Miranda. 2014. *Debt to Society: Accounting for Life under Capitalism*. Minneapolis: University of Minnesota Press.

Kar, Sohini. 2018. *Financializing Poverty: Labor and Risk in Indian Microfinance*. Stanford, CA: Stanford University Press.

Karim, Lamia. 2011. *Microfinance and Its Discontents: Women in Debt in Bangladesh*. Minneapolis: University of Minnesota Press.

Katznelson, Ira. 2005. *When Affirmative Action Was White: An Untold Story of Racial Inequality in Twentieth-Century America*. New York: W. W. Norton.

Keeler, Kasey. 2016. "Putting People Where They Belong: American Indian Housing Policy in the Mid-Twentieth Century." *Native American and Indigenous Studies* 3 (2): 70–104.

Klooster, Daniel. 2013. "The Impact of Trans-National Migration on Commons Management among Mexican Indigenous Communities." *Journal of Latin American Geography* 12 (1): 57–86.

Kray, Christine A. 2006. "Resistance to What? How?: Stalled Social Movements in Cancun." *City & Society : Journal of the Society for Urban Anthropology* 18 (1): 66–89.

Kusno, Abidin. 2013. *After the New Order: Space, Politics, and Jakarta*. Honolulu: University of Hawai'i Press.

Kwak, Nancy H. 2015. *A World of Homeowners: American Power and the Politics of Housing Aid*. Chicago: University of Chicago Press.

Leinaweaver, Jessaca B. 2009. "Raising the Roof in the Transnational Andes: Building Houses, Forging Kinship." *The Journal of the Royal Anthropological Institute* 15 (4): 777–96.

Léonard, Éric, and Bruno Losch. 2009. "La inserción de la agricultura mexicana en el mercado norteamericano: cambios estructurales, mutaciones de la acción pública y recomposición de la economía rural y regional." *Foro Internacional* XLIX(1) (195): 5–46.

Levy, Jonathan. 2012. *Freaks of Fortune: The Emerging World of Capitalism and Risk in America*. Cambridge, MA: Harvard University Press.

Levy Orlik, Noemi, and Christian Domínguez Blancas. 2011. "The Activities and Income Structure of Banks Operating in the Mexican Economy: Have Foreign Multinational Banks Domination in Mexico Modernized the Banking System?" Mexico City: UNAM Research Council.

Lipscomb, Joseph B., John T. Harvey, and Harold Hunt. 2003. "Exchange-Rate Mitigation with Price-Level-Adjusting Mortgages: The Case of the Mexican UDI." *Journal of Real Estate Research* 25 (1): 23–42.

Lobo, Susan. 1982. *A House of My Own: Social Organization in the Squatter Settlements of Lima, Peru*. Tucson: University of Arizona Press.

Lobo, Susan, and Kurt Peters, eds. 2001. *American Indians and the Urban Experience*. Albuquerque, NM: Altamira Press.

Lockhart, James, and Stuart B. Schwartz. 1983. *Early Latin America: A History of Colonial Spanish America and Brazil*. Cambridge: Cambridge University Press.

Loperena, Christopher A. 2017. "Settler Violence? Race and Emergent Frontiers of Progress in Honduras." *American Quarterly* 69 (4): 801–7.

López, Isidro, and Emmanuel Rodríguez. 2011. "The Spanish Model." *New Left Review* 69 (May/June): 5–28.

Lopez, Sarah Lynn. 2015. *The Remittance Landscape: Spaces of Migration in Rural Mexico and Urban USA*. Chicago: University of Chicago Press.

Lovato, Roberto. 2010 (December 3). "Dispatch from Cancun: Developing Paradise in the Suicide Capital." *Colorlines*. https://www.colorlines.com/articles/dispatch-cancun-developing-paradise-suicide-capital.

Lucero, José Antonio. 2008. *Struggles of Voice: The Politics of Indigenous Representation in the Andes*. Pittsburgh: University of Pittsburgh Press.

Macchiavello, Eugenia. 2018. *Microfinance and Financial Inclusion: The Challenge of Regulating Alternative Forms of Finance*. New York: Taylor & Francis.

Macías Richard, Carlos. 1997. *Nueva frontera mexicana: milicia, burocracia y ocupación territorial en Quintana Roo*. Chetumal: Consejo Nacional de Ciencia y Técnologia, Universidad de Quintana Roo.

Mahmud, Tayyab. 2012. "Debt and Discipline." *American Quarterly* 64 (3): 469–94.

Martí, Fernando. 1991. *Cancún: Fantasy of Bankers*. Translated by Jules Siegel. Mexico City: Editora Martí.

Mauss, Marcel. 1967. *The Gift: Forms and Functions of Exchange in Archaic Societies*. New York: Norton.

May, Elaine Tyler. 1988. *Homeward Bound: American Families in the Cold War Era*. New York: Basic Books.

Mbembe, Achille, and Janet Roitman. 1995. "Figures of the Subject in the Time of Crisis." *Public Culture* 7 (2): 323–52.

McCoy Cador, Christine. 2017. *El espejismo de Cancún: análisis del desempeño y evolución de un destino turístico*. Barcelona: Alba Sud Editorial.

McCoy Cador, Christine Elizabeth, and Lorena Hernández von Wobeser, eds. 2020. *Cancún a 50 años de un sueño: Un análisis multidisciplinario de una de las ciudades más jovenes del país*. Mexico City: Editorial Itaca.

McLean, Megan. n.d. *Squatters in Paradise: State-Led Tourism Development in Cancún, 1970–1995*. Unpublished thesis.

Michney, Todd M. 2017. *Surrogate Suburbs: Black Upward Mobility and Neighborhood Change in Cleveland, 1900–1980*. Chapel Hill: University of North Carolina Press.

Mignolo, Walter. 2005. *The Idea of Latin America*. Malden, MA: Blackwell.

Miller, Peter, and Nikolas S. Rose. 2013. *Governing the Present: Administering Economic, Social, and Personal Life*. Cambridge, UK: Polity Press.

Monkkonen, Paavo. 2012. "Housing Finance Reform and Increasing Socioeconomic Segregation in Mexico." *International Journal of Urban and Regional Research* 36 (4): 757–72.

———. 2014. "The Role of Housing Finance in Mexico's Vacancy Crisis." UCLA Ziman Center for Real Estate, Working Paper no. 22. https://www.anderson.ucla.edu/centers /ucla-ziman-center-for-real-estate/research/working-papers.

———. 2018. "Empty Houses across North America: Housing Finance and Mexico's Vacancy Crisis." *Urban Studies* 56 (10): 2075–91.

Moodie, Ellen. 2012. *El Salvador in the Aftermath of Peace: Crime, Uncertainty, and the Transition to Democracy*. Philadelphia: University of Pennsylvania Press.

Moodie, Megan. 2013. "Microfinance and the Gender of Risk: The Case of Kiva.org." *Signs* 38 (2): 279–302.

Moten, Fred. 2013. "The Subprime and the Beautiful." *African Identities* 11(2): 237–45.

Muñoz, Lorena. 2018. "Tianguis as a Possibility of Autogestion: Street Vendors Claim Rights to the City in Cancún, Mexico." *Space and Culture* 21. DOI: 10.1177 /1206331217751776.

Murphy, Edward. 2015. *For a Proper Home: Housing Rights in the Margins of Urban Chile, 1960–2010*. Pittsburgh: University of Pittsburgh Press.

Nader, Laura. 1972. "Up the Anthropologist—Perspectives Gained from Studying Up." In *Reinventing Anthropology*, edited by Dell Hymes, 284–311. New York: Pantheon Books.

Nash, June. 2006. *Practicing Ethnography in a Globalizing World: An Anthropological Odyssey.* Lanham, MD: AltaMira Press.

Negrín, Diana. 2019. *Racial Alterity, Wixarika Youth Activism and the Right to the Mexican City.* Tucson: University of Arizona Press.

Neuwirth, Robert. 2006. *Shadow Cities: A Billion Squatters, A New Urban World.* New York: Routledge.

Ng'weno, Bettina. 2007. *Turf Wars: Territory and Citizenship in the Contemporary State.* Stanford, CA: Stanford University Press.

———. 2012. "Beyond Citizenship as We Know It: Race and Ethnicity in Afro-Colombian Struggles for Citizenship Equality." In *Comparative Perspectives on Afro-Latin America,* edited by Kwame Dixon and John Burdick, 156–75. Gainesville: University Press of Florida.

Nonini, Donald M. 2006. "Introduction: The Global Idea of 'the Commons.'" *Social Analysis* 50 (3): 164–77.

Nuijten, Monique. 2003. *Power, Community and the State: The Political Anthropology of Organisation in Mexico.* London: Pluto Press.

O'Brien, Jean M. 2010. *Firsting and Lasting: Writing Indians out of Existence in New England.* Minneapolis: University of Minnesota Press.

O'Rourke, Kathryn E. 2017. *Modern Architecture in Mexico City: History, Representation, and the Shaping of a Capital.* Pittsburgh: University of Pittsburgh Press.

OECD. 2004. *OECD Reviews of Regulatory Reform: Mexico 2004: Progress in Implementing Regulatory Reform.* Ukraine: OECD.

———. 2015. *Mexico: Transforming Urban Policy and Housing Finance.* Paris: OECD.

Otero, Gerardo. 1996. "Neoliberal Reform and Politics in Mexico: An Overview." In *Neoliberalism Revisited: Economic Restructuring and Mexico's Political Future,* edited by Gerardo Otero, 1–25. Boulder, CO: Westview.

Park, K-Sue. 2016. "Money, Mortgages, and the Conquest of America." *Law and Social Inquiry* 41 (4): 1006–35.

Penglase, Ben. 2014. *Living with Insecurity in a Brazilian Favela: Urban Violence and Daily Life.* New Brunswick, NJ: Rutgers University Press.

Perlman, Janice. 2010. *Favela: Four Decades of Living on the Edge in Rio de Janeiro.* Oxford: Oxford University Press.

Pineda, Baron. 2017. "Indigenous Pan-Americanism: Contesting Settler Colonialism and the Doctrine of Discovery at the UN Permanent Forum on Indigenous Issues." *American Quarterly* 69 (4): 823-832.

Porter, Libby, and Janice Barry. 2016. *Planning for Coexistence? Recognizing Indigenous Rights through Land-Use Planning in Canada and Australia.* London: Routledge.

Postero, Nancy. 2006. *Now We Are Citizens: Indigenous Politics in Postmulticultural Bolivia.* Stanford, CA: Stanford University Press.

———. 2017. *The Indigenous State: Race, Politics, and Performance in Plurinational Bolivia.* Oakland: University of California Press.

Priest, Claire. 2006. "Creating an American Property Law: Alienability and Its Limits in American History." *Harvard Law Review* 120 (2): 385–459.

Programa Universitario de Estudios sobre la Ciudad. Universidad Nacional Autónoma de México (PUEC-UNAM). 2013. *México, Perfil del sector de la vivienda.* Mexico: UN-Habitat, CONAVI. https://www.puec.unam.mx/index.php/publicaciones/145-public aciones-digitales/pd-instituciones/146-mexico-perfil-del-sector-de-la-vivienda

Purnell, Jennie. 1999. "With All Due Respect: Popular Resistance to the Privatization of Communal Lands in Nineteenth-Century Michoacán." *Latin American Research Review* 34 (1): 85–121.

Quijano, Anibal. 2000. "Coloniality of Power, Eurocentrism, and Latin America." *Nepantla* 1 (3): 533–80.

Radcliffe, Sarah A. 2015. *Dilemmas of Difference: Indigenous Women and the Limits of Postcolonial Development Policy.* Durham, NC: Duke University Press.

Rahman, Aminur. 1999. *Women and Microcredit in Rural Bangladesh: An Anthropological Study of Grameen Bank Lending.* Boulder, CO: Westview.

Ramirez, Renya K. 2007a. *Native Hubs: Culture, Community, and Belonging in Silicon Valley and Beyond.* Durham, NC: Duke University Press.

———. 2007b. "Race, Tribal Nation and Gender: A Native Feminist Approach to Belonging." *Meridians* 7(2): 22-40.

Ramos, Alcida Rita. 1998. *Indigenism: Ethnic Politics in Brazil.* Madison: University of Wisconsin Press.

Re Cruz, Alicia. 1996a. "The Thousand and One Faces of Cancun." *Urban Anthropology* 25 (3): 283–310.

———. 1996b. *The Two Milpas of Chan Kom: A Study of Socioeconomic and Political Transformations in a Maya Community.* Albany: State University of New York Press.

———. 2003. "Milpa as an Ideological Weapon: Tourism and Maya Migration to Cancun." *Ethnohistory* 50 (3): 489–502.

Redclift, Michael. 2005. "'A Convulsed and Magic Country': Tourism and Resource Histories in the Mexican Caribbean." *Environment and History* 11 (1): 83–97.

Reddy, Rekha, Miriam Bruhn, and Congyan Tan. 2013. *Financial Capability in Mexico: Results from a National Survey on Financial Behaviors, Attitudes and Knowledges.* Washington, DC: The World Bank.

Redfield, Robert. 1941. *The Folk Culture of Yucatan.* Chicago: The University of Chicago Press.

Redfield, Robert, and Alfonso Villa Rojas. 1934. *Chan Kom: A Maya Village.* Prospect Heights: Waveland.

Reed, Nelson A. 1964. *The Caste War of Yucatán.* Stanford, CA: Stanford University Press.

———. 1997. "Juan de la Cruz, Venancio Puc, and the Speaking Cross." *The Americas* 53 (4): 497–523.

"The Reform of Article 27 and the Urbanisation of the *Ejido* in Mexico." 1994. *Bulletin of Latin American Research* 13 (3): 327–35.

Restall, Matthew. 1997. *The Maya World: Yucatec Culture and Society, 1550–1850.* Stanford, CA: Stanford University Press.

La Revista Peninsular. 2000. "Reserva territorial y su urbanización." In *Semanario de Información y Análisis Político.* Vol. 562. http://www.larevista.com.mx.

Reyes Ruiz del Cueto, Laura Alejandra. 2013. "Housing Access and Governance: The Case of Densification Efforts in Mexico City, 2001–2012." Master's thesis, Department of Community and Regional Planning, University of Texas Austin. https://repositories.lib .utexas.edu/bitstream/handle/2152/22493/REYESRUIZDELCUETO-THESIS-2013 .pdf.

Robichaux, David. 1988. "Hombre, mujer y la tenencia de la tierra en una comunidad de habla náhuatl de Tlaxcala." In *Las mujeres en el campo*, edited by Josefina Aranda Bezaury, 83–100. Oaxaca: UABJO.

Robson, James P., and Gabriela Lichtenstein. 2013. "Current Trends in Latin American Commons Research." *Journal of Latin American Geography* 12 (1): 5–31.

Roitman, Janet L. 2003. "Unsanctioned Wealth; or, The Productivity of Debt in Northern Cameroon." *Public Culture* 15 (2): 211–37.

———. 2014. *Anti-Crisis*. Durham, NC: Duke University Press.

Roy, Ananya. 2010. *Poverty Capital: Microfinance and the Making of Development*. London: Routledge.

Roy, Ananya, and Nezar AlSayyad, eds. 2004. *Urban Informality: Transnational Perspectives from the Middle East, Latin America, and South Asia*. Oxford, UK: Lexington Books.

Rueda Estrada, Verónica, and Natalia Fiorentini Cañedo. 2015. "Los institutos estatales de vivienda en Quintana Roo, México: entre la vivienda popular y el mercado inmobiliario (1974-2010). In *La empresa pública en México y en América Latina: entre el mercado y el estado*, edited by Guillermo Guajardo and Alejandro Labrador, 119–34. Mexico City: UNAM.

Rugeley, Terry. 1996. *Yucatán's Maya Peasantry and the Origins of the Caste War*. Austin: University of Texas Press.

Rus, Diane L., and Jan Rus. 2014. "Trapped behind the Lines: The Impact of Undocumented Migration, Debt, and Recession on a Tsotsil Community of Chiapas, Mexico, 2002–2012." *Latin American Perspectives* 41 (3): 154–77.

Saldaña-Portillo, María Josefina. 2016. *Indian Given: Racial Geographies across Mexico and the United States*. Durham, NC: Duke University Press.

Salvatorre, Ricardo D. 2008. "The Unsettling Location of a Settler Nation: Argentina, from Settler Economy to Failed Developing Nation." *South Atlantic Quarterly* 107 (4): 755–89.

Sánchez, Rosaura, and Beatrice Pita. 2014. "Rethinking Settler Colonialism." *American Quarterly* 66 (4): 1039–55.

Sandoval-Cervantes, Iván. 2017. "Uncertain Futures: The Unfinished Houses of Undocumented Migrants in Oaxaca, Mexico." *American Anthropologist* 119 (2): 209–22.

Satter, Beryl. 2010. *Family Properties: How the Struggle over Race and Real Estate Transformed Chicago and Urban America*. New York: Metropolitan Books.

Sawyer, Suzana M. 2004. *Crude Chronicles: Indigenous Politics, Multinational Oil, and Neoliberalism in Ecuador*. Durham, NC: Duke University Press.

Schmidt, Samuel. 1991. *The Deterioration of the Mexican Presidency: The Years of Luis Echeverría*. Tucson: University of Arizona Press.

Schwanse, Elvira. 2014. "The Mexican Experience in the Social Housing Sector and Programs for Green Housing." *Journal of Architectural Engineering and Technology* 3 (2). http://dx.doi.org/10.4172/2168-9717.1000124.

Scott, James C. 1985. *Weapons of the Weak: Everyday Forms of Peasant Resistance.* New Haven, CT: Yale University Press.

———. 1998. *Seeing like a State: How Certain Schemes to Improve the Human Condition Have Failed.* New Haven, CT: Yale University Press.

———. 2010. *The Art of Not Being Governed: An Anarchist History of Upland Southeast Asia.* New Haven, CT: Yale University Press.

See, Sarita Echavez. 2012. "Gambling with Debt: Lessons from the Illiterate." *American Quarterly* 64 (3): 495–513.

Seider, Rachel. 2002. "Recognizing Indigenous Law and the Politics of State Formation in Mesoamerica." In *Multiculturalism in Latin America: Indigenous Rights, Diversity and Democracy,* edited by Rachel Seider, 184–207. Basingstoke, Hampshire, UK: Palgrave Macmillan.

Shaw, Justine M., and Jennifer P. Matthews. 2005. *Quintana Roo Archaeology.* Tucson: University of Arizona Press.

Simone, AbdouMaliq. 2004. *For the City Yet to Come: Changing African Life in Four Cities.* Durham, NC: Duke University Press.

Simpson, Audra. 2014. *Mohawk Interruptus: Political Life across the Borders of Settler States.* Durham, NC: Duke University Press.

Simpson, Leanne Betasamosake. 2017. *As We Have Always Done: Indigenous Freedom through Radical Resurgence.* Minneapolis: University of Minnesota Press.

Smith, Linda Tuhiwai. 2012. *Decolonizing Methodologies: Research and Indigenous Peoples.* London: Zed.

Soederberg, Susanne. 2014. *Debtfare States and the Poverty Industry: Money, Discipline and the Surplus Population.* New York: Routledge.

Sommer, Doris. 1993. *Foundational Fictions: The National Romances of Latin America.* Berkeley: University of California Press.

Speed, Shannon. 2008. *Rights in Rebellion: Indigenous Struggle and Human Rights in Chiapas.* Stanford, CA: Stanford University Press.

———. 2017. "Structures of Settler Capitalism in Abya Yala." *American Quarterly* 69 (4): 783–90.

———. 2019. *Incarcerated Stories: Indigenous Women Migrants and Violence in the Settler-Capitalist State.* Chapel Hill: University of North Carolina Press.

Stephen, Lynn. 1996. "Too Little, Too Late? The Impact of Article 27 on Women in Oaxaca." In *Reforming Mexico's Agrarian Reform,* edited by Laura Randall, 289–303. New York: M.E. Sharpe.

———. 1997. *Women and Social Movements in Latin America: Power from Below.* Austin: University of Texas Press.

———. 2013. *We Are the Face of Oaxaca: Testimony and Social Movements.* Durham, NC: Duke University Press.

Stickney, Christy. 2014. "Many Paths to a Home: Emerging Business Models for Latin America and the Caribbean's Base of the Pyramid." Washington, DC: Inter-American Development Bank.

Stiglitz, Joseph E. 2013. *The Price of Inequality: How Today's Divided Society Endangers Our Future*. New York: Norton.

Stoll, David. 2013. *El Norte or Bust: How Migration Fever and Microcredit Produced a Financial Crash in a Latin American Town*. New York: Rowman and Littlefield.

Stout, Noelle. 2016a. "#Indebted: Disciplining the Moral Valence of Mortgage Debt Online." *Cultural Anthropology* 31 (1): 82–106.

———. 2016b. "Petitioning a Giant: Debt, Reciprocity, and Mortgage Modification in the Sacramento Valley." *American Ethnologist* 43 (1): 158–71.

———. 2019. *Dispossessed: How Predatory Bureaucracy Foreclosed on the American Middle Class*. Berkeley: University of California Press.

Sullivan, Paul. 1989. *Unfinished Conversations: Mayas and Foreigners between Two Wars*. Berkeley: University of California Press.

Tang, Eric. 2015. *Unsettled: Cambodian Refugees in the NYC Hyperghetto*. Philadelphia: Temple University Press.

Taylor, Keeanga-Yamahtta. 2019. *Race for Profit: How Banks and the Real Estate Industry Undermined Black Homeownership*. Chapel Hill: University of North Carolina Press.

Thrush, Coll. 2016. *Indigenous London: Native Travelers at the Heart of Empire*. New Haven, CT: Yale University Press.

Trejo, Guillermo. 2012. *Popular Movements in Autocracies: Religion, Repression, and Indigenous Collective Action in Mexico*. Cambridge: Cambridge University Press.

Trouillot, Michel-Rolph. 2001. "The Anthropology of the State in the Age of Globalization: Close Encounters of the Deceptive Kind." *Current Anthropology* 42 (1): 125–38.

Tsing, Anna. 2005. *Friction: An Ethnography of Global Connection*. Princeton, NJ: Princeton University Press.

Tuori, Kaius. 2015. "The Theory and Practice of Indigenous Dispossession in the Late Nineteenth Century: The Saami in the Far North of Europe and the Legal History of Colonialism." *Comparative Legal History* 3 (1): 152–85.

UN-Habitat. 2011. *Housing Finance in Mexico*. Nairobi: UN-Habitat.

———. 2012. *State of the World's Cities 2012/2013*. Nairobi: United Nations Human Settlements Programme.

Varley, Ann. 2007. "Gender and Property Formalization: Conventional and Alternative Approaches." *World Development* 35 (10): 1739–53.

———. 2010. "Modest Expectations: Gender and Property Rights in Mexico." *Law & Society Review* 44 (1): 67–100.

———. 2017. "Property Titles and the Urban Poor: From Informality to Displacement?" *Planning Theory & Practice* 18 (3): 385-404.

Vásquez Castillo, María Teresa. 2004. *Land Privatization in Mexico: Urbanization, Formation of Regions, and Globalization in Ejidos*. New York: Routledge.

Villa Rojas, Alfonso. 1978. *Los elegidos de Dios: Etnografía de los mayas de Quintana Roo*. Mexico: Instituto Nacional Indigenista.

Villagómez, Gina, and Wilbert Pinto. 1997. *Mujer maya y desarrollo rural en Yucatán.* Mérida, Yucatán: Ediciones de la Universidad Autónoma de Yucatán.

Vimalassery, Manu, Juliana Hu Pegues, and Alyosha Goldstein. 2016. "Introduction: Colonial Unknowing." *Theory & Event* 19 (4). https://muse.jhu.edu/article/633283.

Walker, Cameron Jean. 2009. *Heritage or Heresy: Archaeology and Culture on the Maya Riviera.* Tuscaloosa: The University of Alabama Press.

Walker, Louise. 2013. *Waking from the Dream: Mexico's Middle Classes after 1968.* Stanford, CA: Stanford University Press.

Walker, Ryan, Ted Jojola, and David Natcher, eds. 2013. *Reclaiming Indigenous Planning.* Montreal: McGill–Queen's University Press.

Ward, Peter M. 1982. "Introduction and Purpose." In *Self-Help Housing: A Critique,* edited by Peter M. Ward, 1–13. London: Mansell.

———. 1990. "Mexico." In *International Handbook of Housing Policies and Practices,* edited by Willem Van Vliet, 407–36. New York: Greenwood.

———. 1998. *Mexico City.* Chichester, UK: John Wiley and Sons.

Ward, Peter M., Edith R. Jiménez Huerta, and María Mercedes Di Virgilio, eds. 2015. *Housing Policy in Latin American Cities: A New Generation of Strategies and Approaches for UN-Habitat III.* New York: Routledge.

Warman, Arturo. 1980. *"We Come to Object": The Peasants of Morelos and the National State.* Translated by Stephen K Ault. Baltimore: Johns Hopkins University Press.

———. 1985. *Estrategias de sobrevivencia de los campesinos mayas.* Mexico City: UNAM.

Warren, Elizabeth, and Amelia Warren Tyagi. 2007. *The Two-Income Trap: Why Middle-Class Parents Are Going Broke.* New York: Basic Books.

Weismantel, Mary. 2001. *Cholas and Pishtacos: Stories of Race and Sex in the Andes.* Chicago: University of Chicago Press.

Williams, Brett. 2004. *Debt for Sale: A Social History of the Credit Trap.* Philadelphia: University of Pennsylvania Press.

Williams, Raymond. 1977. *The Country and the City.* New York: Oxford University Press.

Wilson, Tamar Diana. 1993. "We Seek Work Where We Can: A Comparison of Patterns of Transnational Outmigration from a Rancho in Jalisco and Internal Migration into a Mexicali Squatter Settlement." *Journal of Borderland Studies* 8 (2): 33–58.

———. 2008. "Economic and Social Impacts of Tourism in Mexico." *Latin American Perspectives* 35 (3): 37–52.

Wolfe, Patrick.1999. *Settler Colonialism and the Transformation of Anthropology.* London: Cassell.

———. 2006. "Settler Colonialism and the Elimination of the Native." *Journal of Genocide Research* 8 (4): 387–409.

Zavisca, Jane R. 2012. *Housing the New Russia.* Ithaca, NY: Cornell University Press.

Zelizer, Viviana A. 2010. *Economic Lives: How Culture Shapes the Economy.* Princeton, NJ: Princeton University Press.

Index

Note: Page numbers in *italics* indicate illustrations.

The authorized representative in the EU for product safety and compliance is:
Mare Nostrum Group
B.V Doelen 72
4831 GR Breda
The Netherlands

www.ingramcontent.com/pod-product-compliance
Lightning Source LLC
Chambersburg PA
CBHW030845270326
41928CB00007B/1223